The TQM TRANSFORMATION

A Model for Organizational Change

Edited by
John Persico, Jr.

QUALITY RESOURCES
A Division of The Kraus Organization Limited
White Plains, New York

Most Quality Resources books are available at quantity discounts when purchased in bulk. For more information contact:

Special Sales Department
Quality Resources
A Division of The Kraus Organization Limited
One Water Street
White Plains, New York 10601
800-247-8519   914-761-9600

Printed in the United States of America
96 95 94 93 92   10 9 8 7 6 5 4 3 2 1

Quality Resources
A Division of The Kraus Organization Limited
One Water Street
White Plains, New York 10601

∞

The paper used in this publication meets the minimum requirements of American National Standard for Information Sciences—Permanence of Paper for Printed Library Materials, ANSI Z39.48-1984.

ISBN 0-527-91654-4

Cover design by Joseph DePinho

Library of Congress Cataloging-in-Publication Data

The TQM transformation : a model for organizational change / edited by
  John Persico, Jr.
      p.   cm.
  Includes bibliographical references and index.
  ISBN 0-527-91654-4 (acid-free paper)
  1. Total quality management.   I. Persico, John.
HD62.15.T78   1992
658.5′62—dc20   92-86
                                                                  CIP

Contents

v

Foreword

Competitiveness in world markets is critical to the well-being of the American industrial enterprise. Competitiveness is enhanced by process improvement and innovation, which are achieved through a focus on quality. The benefits of enhanced quality are reduced re-work, greater productivity, lower unit cost, price flexibility, improved competitive position, increased demand, larger profits, more jobs, and more secure jobs. Customers get high quality at a low price, vendors get predictable long-term sources of business, and investors earn increased profits. Everybody wins. However, if productivity alone is stressed to achieve competitiveness, quality can be sacrificed, and lower output may actually result. Employee morale will plunge, costs will rise, customers will be unhappy, stockholders will be concerned, and competitive position will decline. Everybody loses.

Top management determines the effectiveness and efficiency with which their organizations institutionalize "quality concepts." This book presents a model, in harmony with W. Edwards Deming's theory of management, for the institutionalization of quality concepts in any organization.

Dr. Deming says, "You cannot copy, you must understand why things work." That is exactly why Dr. Deming has not developed a cookbook for all to follow in respect to his theory of management. You must develop your own practices.

This book explains the anatomy of Process Management International's model, which is designed to make Dr. Deming's management theory a reality in your place of work. The book is quite innovative, perhaps even unique, in that it illustrates each component of the PMI model through case studies at PMI's client sites.

The authors believe, and I concur, that studying someone else's theories and practices can be extremely helpful as you develop your own theories and practices.

One word of caution when reading about the application of quality concepts in different companies (case studies). The same company that generates successful case study material also generates failed case study material. So, a reader must recognize that copying case studies may lead to success in one scenario and failure in another. This book avoids the trap of presenting successful case studies for others to copy by setting the case studies in the context of theory.

This book is filled with gems. To mention only one of them, in Chapter 8 there is a discussion of the significance of the relationship between the consultant (from PMI in this case) and the client. The authors point out that it is not necessary for the consultant to become a close friend of the client, but "the consultant must be honest, knowledgeable, ethical, trustworthy, and have the client's interests above his or her own gain." This excellent point highlights the authors' insight into quality management.

This is a wonderful book, and I recommend it to anyone interested in the improvement of quality in business, government, and industry.

Howard S. Gitlow, Ph.D.
Executive Director
Institute for the Study of Quality
   in Manufacturing and Service
University of Miami
Coral Gables, Florida

Introduction: The Transformation Model

LOUIS E. SCHULTZ AND JOHN S. VOLLUM
Process Management International

Total Quality Management—or TQM—means fully utilizing the brainpower of each and every employee. It is the systematic elimination of waste and rework created by imperfect processes. It is an appreciation of the variation inherent in processes. It is an understanding that all an organization's efforts are part of a system, and that you cannot change one part of the system without affecting the other parts.

This book is about a model for TQM, a model for transforming organizations and creating a workplace that supports the quest for quality and continuous improvement. It will help managers understand a process by which they can begin the transformation effort in their own organizations. The story of how this can be done is told not by Process Management International, the consulting firm that has developed the model, but by managers and employees who have adapted the model to their own organizations.

Process Management International (PMI) was founded in 1984 as a privately owned business dedicated to promoting the concept of TQM and the philosophy of Dr. W. Edwards Deming in American industry. In September of 1985, executives of Zytec Corporation, a Minnesota-based designer and manufacturer of power supplies for the information processing industry, sought help for their faltering quality program. Two consultants, Gary N. McLean, a University of Minnesota professor of training and organizational development, and Samuel Pakenham-Walsh, an organizational development consultant with PMI, offered Zytec their combined knowledge and expertise in return for using Zytec as a "laboratory" for organizational change. From this partnership, the transformation model was born (McLean and Pakenham-Walsh 1987).

As PMI has prospered, it has forged links with quality consulting organizations in Japan, England, Europe, China, South America, and Malaysia. Each of these relationships has enabled the company to increase its knowledge of TQM and broaden its strategies and techniques for helping organizations make the quality transformation. PMI's growth and development, together with the maturation of its clients, has resulted in the continuous improvement and refinement of the model. Evidence of this may be seen in the efforts of Zytec, which received the Malcolm Baldrige National Quality Award in 1991.

Historically, organizational change efforts have focused primarily on structural or technical change. These efforts, however, are often unsuccessful, because they fail to recognize that organizational structural and technical systems are dynamically linked with human behavior. The philosophy of Dr. Deming addresses this integration of structural, technical, and human elements, and the transformation model uses his ideas as a place to start the quality journey.

The unique aspect of this model is that it provides a structure that can be adapted to most types of manufacturing and service organizations. It is not, however, a cookbook or recipe that tells managers how to implement quality or what they must do each day of the transformation. As Dr. Deming says, you cannot copy, you must understand *why* something works.

The inherent openness of the PMI model—its need to be translated or adapted—is probably the most difficult part for managers who are used to black-and-white procedures or specifications. In addition, many managers challenge the applicability of the model, arguing that "it won't work here because we are different." It is true that no two organizations are alike, but proof that the model can work is seen in the diverse types of organizations represented in this book.

Those who are familiar with quality terminology will recognize the concept of the Shewhart PDCA Cycle embedded in the model. This concept is based on a never-ending cycle of Plan–Do–Check–

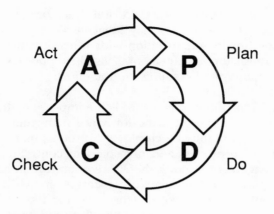

FIGURE A.1   The PDCA cycle.

Act (Figure A.1). New concepts are planned, implemented on a pilot basis, studied, and the positive aspects are incorporated into the model. This process is not complete and is far from perfect, which is evident from the procedures and experiences described by the authors. Nevertheless, one essential feature of the model remains unchanged: its reliance on the expertise of an organization's employees and managers to adapt and tailor the model to their unique business and culture.

Several beliefs are fundamental to success with this model. Because they run counter to some common beliefs, they should be stated explicitly:

- People want to do a good job. They do not begin employment expecting to do poorly. Believing that people want to do a good job means that most often (Deming says 93 percent of the time) their performance is affected more by the *systems* in which they work rather than solely by their particular skills, abilities, or motivation. Managers who know this can more productively spend their time understanding the system from which problems arise, rather than assigning blame to individuals.
- Process (*how* things are done) is more crucial, though not more important, than results. Results are important to any organization, but it is more critical to understand and act on the process that produces the results if long-term improvement is to occur.

- Senior management must lead the transformation. While isolated, limited successes may be achieved within small groups or departments, organization-wide transformation will not succeed unless top management is visibly supportive and commits time, energy, and resources to the effort.

A critical function in this regard is the implementation of process management. As opposed to performance management, which focuses on efforts to motivate employees, process management looks at controlling the process and not solely at controlling employees. Process management regards the entire organization as one system that is composed of a number of processes, in which the human element is only one of several factors affecting the outcome (Figure A.2). Only by continually improving all critical processes can the organization continue to prosper.

To see an organization as a system that is composed of vast numbers of processes also means a shift to a more cross-functional view of business, looking at major processes as they cross departmental or functional boundaries. Hiring, budgeting, and purchasing, for example, may be processes that are usually the primary responsibility of a specific department, yet they often involve and affect people from several departments. A process view shows the need for coordination and cooperative management and communication. It also entails defining the process owner to establish ac-

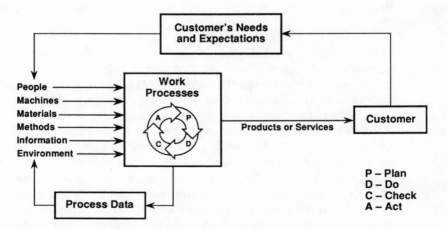

FIGURE A.2   A process view of organizations.

countability, and defining and monitoring critical processes, quality measures, and customer requirements.

OVERVIEW OF THE TRANSFORMATION MODEL

The transformation model provides a structure for the roles and responsibilities in a TQM effort. These roles include all levels of managers and employees (Figure A.3):

- The Executive Steering Committee, including the CEO, leads and supports the transformation for the entire organization.
- Local Steering Committees lead the transformation and improvement efforts in their individual business units.
- The TQM Coordinator is the focal point for all TQM activities in the organization.
- Quality Leadership Teams study organizational barriers to TQM and identify areas that need to be addressed.
- Process Improvement (PI) Advisors teach statistical process control (SPC) and other process improvement methods, and help teams use these tools.

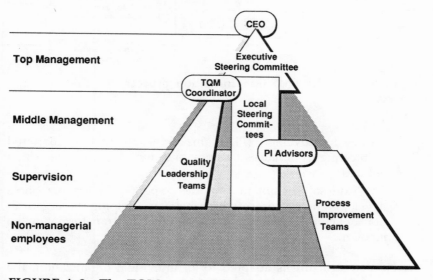

FIGURE A.3   The TQM organizational structure.

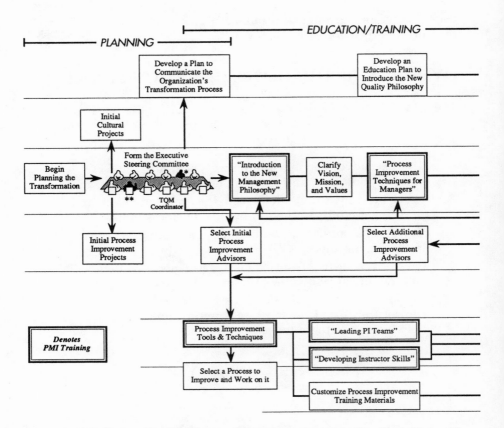

FIGURE A.4   The PMI transformation process: the first 10 to 15 months.

- Process Improvement (PI) Teams are groups that are chartered by Steering Committees to study and improve processes within defined areas.
- The external consultant provides expertise in organizational development and process improvement, helping the organization develop the resources to continue the transformation on its own.

As this structure is adapted to an individual organization, the names of the teams (or committees or units), as well as the team

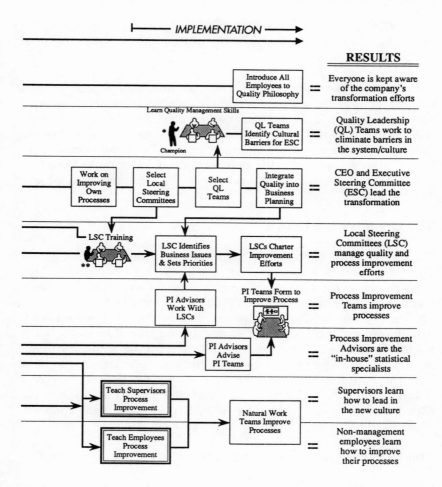

leaders (or owners or champions), may be changed to provide a unique organizational signature to the effort.

The interrelationships among these players and the results of their efforts can be seen in Figure A.4, which illustrates the four basic stages in the model:

1. Planning (1 to 3 months).
2. Education (3 to 36 months).
3. Implementation (starts with planning and begins to increase rapidly after about the 15th month).

4. Continuous improvement (begins about month 36, although the organization is not likely to be fully in this mode until after the fifth year of the effort).

Although the model begins with planning, this element continues throughout the entire effort. Similarly, there is an element of education at each stage. The actual time that it takes to go through these stages depends on a number of factors, such as the size of the organization, the resources allocated to the effort, the commitment by top management, and the perceived need for change. Most theorists estimate three to five years for an organization to adapt to a TQM culture.

The Organization Leader

The role of the CEO or organization leader is described in Chapter 1 by Mr. Lorne Ames, president of the Manitoba Division of Inco Limited, one of the largest mining companies in the world. Mr. Ames started the transformation effort at Inco-Manitoba in 1986.

The organization leader is perhaps the single most important factor in determining the success or failure of the transformation. If the leader is not an actively involved role model for the effort, it will not be successful. Proof of this is seen in the success of those who have won the Malcolm Baldrige Award. In each case, the presence of a strong and dedicated leader is highly evident. This firmly places the expectation of leadership at the highest level and avoids compartmentalization (or departmentalization) of quality.

The Executive Steering Committee

The role of the Executive Steering Committee is described in Chapter 2, which is written by the Executive Steering Committee for the Western Canada Structural Division of Dominion Bridge, one of the oldest and largest steel construction and fabrication companies in North America. The division is headed by Mr. A. Wayne Stewart, senior vice president, who formed the Committee in 1987.

The purpose of the Executive Steering Committee is to plan, lead, support, and continuously improve the transformation effort. The Committee is led by the organization leader and includes the managers who directly report to him or her. Other managers or employees may also be members of the Committee, so that the entire organization is represented. For example, other major groups, such as union leadership, physicians in hospitals, boards of directors, and so on, should be represented.

The Committee should have a facilitator (not the leader) to assist with team start-up and planning, the continuing education of the senior managers, and ongoing issues of organizational development. Initially, the facilitator should be an external consultant with whom the team is comfortable. In later stages, the facilitator's job can be taken over by the internal TQM Coordinator.

Because of its leadership role, it is important to form the Committee early. Senior management must be out front in terms of understanding quality principles, planning the transformation, and identifying early resources, such as the TQM Coordinator and some initial Process Improvement (PI) Advisors. The Committee then selects and begins one or more initial projects to develop their confidence in the use of process improvement tools and methods. This early project work also serves to provide examples that can be used in educating the rest of the organization.

Since senior managers are watched closely by the rest of the organization, they have the opportunity to be role models, showing that they really believe in TQM and that it is worth the effort, even though it may not be easy to change years of traditional managing habits. The Committee must visibly support change efforts, working to create an atmosphere for change and a learning environment. This includes planning and supporting opportunities for all employees to learn and use quality principles and techniques, promoting teamwork, and recognizing teams and individuals for their efforts.

Clarifying the organization's mission, vision, and values is an important step in the Committee's work. The mission and vision statements provide a framework for identifying TQM priorities and planning a strategy for action at every level in the organization. The Committee can then begin to charter Local Steering Committees within individual business units. Because the Committee represents the entire organization, it is also in the ideal position to promote and coordinate activities that cross department or division boundaries.

In the long term, the Committee's activities evolve from managing the business *and* the transformation effort, to managing the business *with* the transformation effort integrated into all activities.

Local Steering Committees

The role of the Local Steering Committee is described in Chapter 3 by Mr. Lawrence Lucchesi from the Olefins and Derivatives Division of Chevron Chemical Company. Mr. Lucchesi is the plant manager for the Cedar Bayou plant, which produces derivative chemicals used in a wide variety of consumer products. As leader of the plant's Local Steering Committee, Mr. Lucchesi is responsible for coordinating the plant's improvement activities with the division's Executive Steering Committee.

The Local Steering Committee works under the guidance of the Executive Steering Committee to establish the philosophy and methodology of continual process improvement in a particular business unit. This may be a division, plant, department, or other functional unit. Depending on its structure and geographical dispersion, an organization may establish one or several Local Steering Committees.

TQM often begins with one or two business units that are either ready to start, are geographically close to corporate offices, are small enough to be considered a pilot, or are traditionally more open to change. It is not necessary for all business units to begin at once. In fact, it is sometimes better to wait and learn from the experience of one carefully monitored implementation.

The leader of the Local Steering Committee is the business unit manager and, in most cases, is also a member of the Executive Steering Committee, thus creating a vital link for support and communication. The other members of the Committee are those who report directly to the unit manager, a union management representative where applicable, and additional functional representatives as needed. The Committee should also have a facilitator (not the leader) to assist with their continuing education, team start-up and planning, and ongoing issues of organizational development. Initially, the facilitator should be a consultant with whom the team is comfortable. Later, the position may be filled by an internal PI Advisor.

The Local Steering Committee's task is to identify specific opportunities for process improvement at the work level, charter PI Teams to address these issues, and select the people who need to be involved in the process. The Committee members themselves must learn to use and integrate process improvement tools and methods in day-to-day operations. Members must visibly support process improvement activities and foster the involvement of all employees in those activities. Because members of the Committee may already meet in the course of their regular work, their quality efforts eventually become a part of their normal business activities.

The Local Steering Committee must establish priorities for its process improvement efforts. It may charter the first PI Teams to focus on chronic problems and/or current headaches. Later, the priorities for improvement efforts are driven by the business planning process, which identifies the factors and processes that are most critical for the ongoing success of the business unit.

One of the Committee's most critical functions is to create and execute a plan for employee education in quality principles and process improvement tools and methods. Training should accommodate both formal classroom instruction and just-in-time education, which is classroom-centered but oriented to current, real-life projects in the workplace. Another aspect of education is the mentoring or coaching relationship that is often vital to help middle managers change their management styles. Training and educating the workforce can be capital-intensive, and it must be a stable, carefully planned process; it cannot rely on one person training another, who in turn trains another. Establishing PI Teams and developing internal PI Advisors to handle the bulk of this training can help ensure stability and reduce costs considerably.

TQM Coordinator

The role of the TQM Coordinator is described in Chapter 4 by Mr. Gerry Damon from Pearl Harbor Naval Shipyard (PHNSY), which overhauls and refits both surface ships and nuclear submarines. PHNSY started on a full-fledged TQM effort in 1986. Mr. Damon, a mechanical engineer who has worked for the Navy for over twenty years, was appointed TQM Coordinator shortly after PHNSY became involved in TQM.

The TQM Coordinator is usually a middle- or higher-level manager who is appointed full-time to coordinate the planning, implementation, and continuous improvement of the TQM effort. The Coordinator is a member of the Executive Steering Committee and reports directly to the CEO or senior manager. The term "coordinator" is carefully chosen, because the responsibility for the transformation remains that of senior management; it should not be delegated to the Coordinator. The Coordinator should, however, be the designated and highly visible internal agent for change.

As the focal point for all the organization's TQM activities, the Coordinator's typical responsibilities are to:

- Work closely with PI Advisors and PI Teams in need of facilitation and other process improvement assistance.

- Draft and revise the transformation plan with the Executive Steering Committee.
- Coordinate education and training for the entire organization.
- Act as the liaison and contractor for consulting services.
- Build organizational awareness about the TQM effort.

The appointment of the Coordinator should be made early enough so that the person has the time to get out in front of the effort and acquire a comprehensive working knowledge of TQM principles, tools, techniques, and team leadership and facilitation skills. Because the Coordinator is also the primary liaison with outside consulting services, he or she should be named in time to participate in the selection process.

Quality Leadership Teams

The role of Quality Leadership Teams is described in Chapter 5 by Mr. John Rogers, vice president of finance at Zytec Corporation. Zytec, which manufactures power supplies for the computer industry, began its quality transformation in 1985. Zytec was both the first recipient of the Minnesota Quality Award and one of only three winners of the Malcolm Baldrige Award in 1991. Mr. Rogers was the leader of one of the first Quality Leadership Teams.

Quality Leadership Teams address the organization's culture with the aim to improve management leadership and create an environment that supports the efforts of all employees. These teams are typically "diagnostic": they focus on identifying system-wide barriers to the transformation that are embedded in company policies and procedures. Their specific targets are the processes that are traditionally the province of management, such as performance appraisals, salary incentives, hiring procedures, training policies, budgeting, and safety.

Quality Leadership Teams may be chartered either by the Executive Steering Committee, or the Local Steering Committee if the area of study is within their unit. They usually consist of managers (including union management where appropriate) from several levels and departments, making the teams multi-level and cross-functional.

There are two common strategies for Quality Leadership Teams. The first is to divide the Fourteen Points (see Appendix A) into thematic areas, such as philosophy, policies, and practices, and then form teams to identify organizational barriers in each of these areas. A second strategy is to identify a specific issue or problem area, such as schedule changes that cut across departmental lines, and then charter a team to diagnose the problem. Because most Quality Leadership Teams do not have the expertise and representation to define and implement their recommended changes, the Steering Committee may charter a PI Team to address the recommendations.

Quality Leadership Teams have been an excellent training vehicle for managers in learning and exercising data-supported, bottom–up authority, in which the traditional top–down organizational pyramid is inverted (Figure A.5). The teams, however, do face a difficult task. It is unknown territory for most members because the normal hierarchy is dissolved as much as possible, and some may find they have more (or less) influence than they had before. Also, they may be given large and complex problems that, upon analysis, seem interconnected with everything in the organization. This is in the nature of systemic problems or barriers. Because of the potential for frustration, the Steering Committee must give great care and attention to nurturing these teams.

Process Improvement (PI) Advisors

The role of the PI Advisor is described in Chapter 6 by Mr. Michael Thomas from Chevron Pipe Line Company (CPL), a subsidiary of Chevron Corporation. CPL operates and maintains over 11,000 miles of pipeline in the United States, handling the transfer of petroleum liquids, chemicals, and gas from production fields to refining centers to marketing distribution terminals. Mr. Thomas, a registered professional engineer and currently a district superintendent, was selected as the TQM Coordinator when CPL started its transformation effort in 1988.

PI Advisors are key people who advise and instruct teams and individuals in using process improvement methods in their day-to-day work. This role can progress from that of advisor to that of an instructor and, finally, to that of an internal consultant. The PI Advisor is a transitional role, although it may continue for several years. As process improvement skills are transferred to more individuals, the Advisor's role is assumed by managers.

There are usually several PI Advisors in an organization, depending on its size and distribution. The Executive Steering Com-

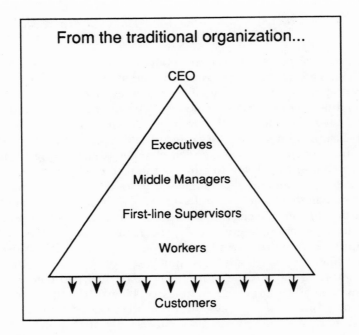

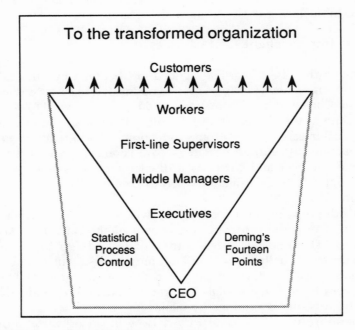

FIGURE A.5   The inverted pyramid.

mittee needs to identify at least one Advisor to work on the initial projects that kick off the TQM effort. Later, as Local Steering Committees are chartered, they select and train PI Advisors for work in their units.

Advisors can be hourly or salaried employees (even managers, in some cases), who have an affinity for numbers, good people skills, and excellent credibility. After receiving in-depth training in basic statistical tools and team effectiveness, they work with a Local Steering Committee to identify specific opportunities for improvement. PI Advisors can be helped greatly by a consultant who coaches and assists with the Advisor's first assignments. As PI Teams are formed, the Advisor trains and advises team members and other employees in the use of SPC. The Advisor is not a team leader, but may help with team start-up and coordination.

Process Improvement (PI) Teams

The role of PI Teams is described in Chapter 7 by the Training and Education Department at H. M. Smyth Company, and Ms. Dawn Sorenson. H. M. Smyth, one of the oldest established printing firms in Minnesota, embarked on its TQM transformation in 1987.

PI Teams address the improvement of specific processes related to increasing customer satisfaction. The teams are chartered by the Executive or Local Steering Committees to address either functional issues within a department or unit, or cross-functional issues that cross departmental or unit boundaries. The majority of teams are chartered by Local Steering Committees as they identify business priorities and problem areas. A typical charter specifies an area of focus, which the PI Team further defines given its unique process knowledge.

The typical PI Team is composed of six to eight employees who are trained in SPC and team effectiveness. Team membership is highly dependent on the particular process being studied. Ideally, a team includes those who work in the process, the internal and/or external suppliers and customers of the process, the supervisor of the process, and a facilitator as required. PI Teams may last from six weeks to six months, depending on the scope and magnitude of the issue, and disband when they complete their work and report back to the Steering Committee.

This model stresses team activities, because a properly constituted team enjoys the power of pooled abilities and the associated benefits of communication, community, and broader ownership of changes. Not all improvement activities require a PI Team, however; because many improvements do come from individuals, the Local Steering Committee should also find ways to nurture and respond to the ideas of individuals.

The External Consultant

The role of the external consultant is described in Chapter 8 by Dr. John Persico and Dr. Sharon Loubert of PMI. Both consultants have been with PMI since 1986, and have worked with a wide range of clients in service and manufacturing industries. Dr. Persico's expertise is in organizational development, and Dr. Loubert's expertise is in statistics.

The external consultant guides the organization, helping it develop its own internal resources to continue the transformation. Consultants fill a number of roles with the client, serving as meeting facilitators, trainers, and coaches. The ideal consultant has skills in both organizational development and SPC. Because consultants rarely have expertise in both these areas, PMI uses two consultants at each client site.

The organizational development (OD) consultant works with senior management on the development of the organization's resources. While most organizations prepare well for growth, few spend the time needed to develop resources such as personnel, planning systems, communication systems, and training. The OD consultant focuses on a strategy for resource development and addresses the areas of leadership skills, long-term vision and planning, labor-management cooperation, training and education, constancy of purpose, and an environment conducive to creativity and risk-taking.

The Process Improvement (PI) consultant's role is to demonstrate and teach statistical thinking and methodology. The consultant works with the Steering Committees, PI Advisors, and PI Teams on process issues. The consultant assists the PI Advisors until they become comfortable in their roles, and sometimes acts as an expert advisor when a greater degree of statistical sophistication is needed.

Union Participation

The importance of a union–management partnership is discussed in Chapter 9 by Mr. Robert Killeen, who has been active in labor relations for over forty years. He is a past sub-regional director of the UAW for Minnesota, and serves on the board of the Twin Cities Labor Management Council and the Minnesota Council for Quality.

Although you can have labor-management participation without TQM, you cannot have TQM without labor-management participation. In many industries, the union represents a vital and potent element in the organization, and has the right to be involved in any and all changes that may affect the working conditions or safety of employees.

The traditional adversarial relationship between labor and management must be abandoned if TQM is to succeed. Involving the union as an equal partner right from the start is a first step in bringing about a new level of cooperation and commitment. The heart, if not the soul, of TQM is the concept of total employee involvement and empowerment. These concepts are not mere buzzwords, but a way of life in those organizations where TQM is successful.

For most, embarking on a quality transformation means change, not only for our organizations but also for ourselves. It means changing the way we perceive management and managing, and changing the way we see ourselves as managers and workers. Developing the ability to see ourselves and our organizations differently is fundamental to the success of transformation efforts. Perhaps Marcel Proust said it best: "The real voyage of discovery lies not in seeking new landscapes but in having new eyes."

TQM can work in any industry, business, or organization. Once the focus shifts from the product or service to the *process*, then the fundamental concepts of TQM become relevant everywhere. I hope the reader will gain some insight into how to implement TQM by seeing the problems that others have faced and the knowledge they have acquired. This book is written by the people who have been there.

1

The Organization Leader

LORNE M. AMES
Inco Limited

The organization leader (usually the CEO) has the greatest leverage in determining the success or failure of the transformation effort. He or she must be persistent, dedicated, and fully committed to TQM. The leader should be a member of the Executive Steering Committee, and must be actively involved in the effort as a role model, providing the leadership, encouragement, support, and resources that the organization needs, and keeping the pursuit of quality at the very highest level of expectation among senior management (Figure 1.1). At the same time, it is folly to consider the leader as somehow able to accomplish a transformation of this magnitude without the encouragement, support, and resources of the organization itself. The leader, like everyone else, is a member of the team.

This chapter describes the role and recounts the experiences of the organization leader at the Manitoba Division of Inco Limited.

PROFILE: INCO LIMITED, MANITOBA DIVISION

The Manitoba Division of Inco Limited is based in Thompson, Manitoba. Its main products are electrolytic nickel slab and proprietary

1

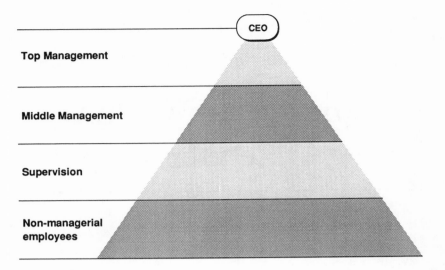

FIGURE 1.1

nickel rounds. The operation consists of two underground mines, an open pit, a mill, a smelter, and an electrolytic refinery.

Before 1986, the two thousand employees of the Manitoba Division focused on cost and productivity improvement to survive the continuing, devastatingly low prices for its nickel products through the 1980s. Nickel prices collapsed from $3.14 per pound in 1980, to a low of $1.94 in 1986, as market volumes retreated in the face of world recession. An industry shakeout saw many nickel producers leave the business entirely.

At Inco, production levels fell as producers struggled to balance supply with demand. Workforce levels fell even further as labor productivity doubled through the introduction of new mining equipment and processes, new higher-grade and lower-cost open-pit mines, metallurgical advances, and automation. Production costs declined for six consecutive years. During this period, corporate philosophy and attitudes shifted to a healthy dissatisfaction with the status quo. If product prices could not be controlled, product costs certainly could.

The challenge in 1986, the year the division "discovered" quality, was how to achieve further improvement. Other units of the company were being encouraged by customers to adopt statistical process control (SPC) to guarantee product quality. This encouragement might have come to naught, had it not been for a brochure announcing a four-day Deming seminar on quality, productivity, and competitive advantage. The brochure described ways to achieve unheard-of levels of employee involvement. It promoted the importance of statistical thinking and referred to successful Japanese management techniques.

At a seminar in Washington, Dr. Deming directly challenged our current management practices: "You don't even know what your job is!" He laid out his solution to American industrial malaise in profound but simple principles that seemed strange and even provocative. Does improved quality really reduce costs? Can fear and barriers within a corporation really be crippling? Is process variation really that important? Are over ninety percent of mistakes really management's fault—therefore *my* fault—in accepting work processes that are designed to produce inferior products? We struggled with these concepts and over time became convinced of their fundamental truth.

The division has now been involved in the pursuit of quality for five years. We often felt that we had turned the corner, only to find more obstacles and more challenges. It has seemed painstakingly slow. Efforts have had to be continuously revised, and it is only upon looking back that we see the tremendous change. It has not been an easy road, but it has been the right one.

THE ROLE OF THE LEADER

The most exciting and challenging event in one's career can begin with the decision to embark on the road to quality. An introduction to the philosophy of quality can open the door to real leadership—giving people the help and opportunity to bring out the best in themselves. Dr. Deming's philosophy, his strong sense of morality, as evidenced by his deep respect for people, his belief that employees must find joy in their work, and his application of statistical thinking to all organizational processes—all combined to offer a new and promising approach to the management of our division.

Much of this excitement became widely shared, albeit with a great deal of uncertainty as to how to make it all happen. To "enlightened" people it seemed natural. Who is against quality? But now there was a road map, or so we thought.

It was obvious that with the pursuit of quality as a management philosophy encompassing every aspect of the organization, and with its apparent success elsewhere, a powerful tool had been discovered. As leader, my ownership of these quality principles would be crucial. Promoting positive management principles would drive the organization forward, or with probably greater ease, its progress could be squelched through either inappropriate action or inaction.

As the leader, one must have the initiative and commitment to:

- *Include the pursuit of quality in the performance expectations of all units of the business.* The leader establishes performance expectations for the organization. At Inco, these entail safety, production, product quality, productivity, and costs, as well as environmental standards and public and government relations—all of these within both annual and long-term time frames. Performance expectations are high, and achieving them is always important. These expectations now include the pursuit of quality and the use of SPC for continuous improvement.

- *Break down interdepartmental barriers.* Breaking down barriers requires the leader's initiative. We became more aware of friction, lack of understanding, and missed opportunities resulting from barriers between work groups. Previously, such barriers had not been seen as a problem of any consequence. Opportunities for improvement appeared everywhere as cross-functional initiatives began to take hold and all eighteen departments, both line and functional, began discussing their interdependencies.

- *Influence people to embrace the quality movement.* The leader is in a position to influence people to embrace the movement to quality. It was difficult to respect the right of individuals to be reluctant to join in. Obviously, the leader should not ride roughshod over such skepticism. Change is never easy, and resistance to change is natural and to be expected. But by helping people recognize there is a better way, they can be recruited and involved in the discovery and ownership of that better way.

- *Anchor the transformation, protecting it from internal and external pressures.* The leader's total commitment is needed to anchor the transformation and allow it to grow, protecting it from internal and external pressures. Pressures from the outside always exist, particularly to improve short-term performance, sometimes with unfavorable impact on long-term performance. By recognizing this, and by ensuring that long-term investment in people and process development is made, an appropriate balance can be sought. Maintaining this balance was, and will continue to be for some time, a difficult burden for us. Given time, the application of quality principles and statistical thinking can improve unit performance and relieve external pressures.

Although this chapter highlights the role of the organization leader, considerable success can be achieved at other levels in any enlightened organization. Leaders, formal and informal, at all levels of an organization, can use quality principles and SPC to improve performance. Local successes can grow to envelop the entire organization.

THE ROAD TO QUALITY

Deming's four-day seminar made evident the tremendous potential to improve our organization's performance. Training and education were our first priorities. Within six months, all department heads attended the seminars in small groups. Meanwhile, many books on quality and SPC were studied, and libraries were established in each area. This early training provided a common base. Together, our management team struggled to assimilate Deming's concepts. This struggle to understand developed our team spirit and commitment to the common goal.

A consultant with a reputation for good knowledge of quality principles was hired to teach the use of SPC. We recognized at the outset that the consultant could not "deliver" Deming and SPC, but would act more as a guide and partner. The consultant could not substitute for my and the organization's discovering our own solutions: most improvement would come from self-discovery. The consultant provided one- and two-day introductory seminars for all supervisors on the principles of quality. Later, this training was assumed by the division with the appointment of TQM Coordinators. Although the consultant's role diminished as implementation progressed, the relationship endures.

Steering Committee

With our consultant's advice, we established an Executive Steering Committee composed of ten senior managers from the larger departments to lead and coordinate the pursuit of quality. From the beginning, this Steering Committee has kept the pursuit of quality at the very highest level of expectation among senior management. Members help select agenda topics for these weekly two-hour meetings. The agenda has evolved from theoretical quality management techniques to current issues and practical processes for integrating quality principles into major objectives, such as production and costs. Subcommittees are sometimes formed to study certain issues in detail.

Quality Leadership Teams

There was initial confusion about how Deming's Fourteen Points related to our division. What did the first principle (constancy of purpose) mean to us? What was this new leadership? Did we have fear in our division? If so, was it debilitating, and what could we do about it? How would we even recognize pride and satisfaction, and how might we go about encouraging it? What were the barriers between working groups?

Three subcommittees (Quality Leadership Teams) of ten members each were set up to study Deming's principles, determine their relevance to the division, and make recommendations for implementation. One team focused on management principles, one on policies, and one on practices.

These teams included all senior management and a cross-section of salaried employees. They struggled with Deming's principles and were effective in forming a critical mass of knowledge in their respective work areas. Whenever an apparent conflict between our established policies and procedures and the quality principles surfaced, we relied on the deliberations of the subcommittees to produce recommendations. The teams were disbanded after two years, and although a game plan to address each of the principles was never developed, the members did become familiar with their meaning and importance. One has to start somewhere, and this route worked. The members, including senior management, became the voice for the pursuit of quality.

Commitment to Quality

Deming's Fourteen Points were translated to our own pursuit of quality, so that they could be put into practice in the division. To capture the essential ingredients of the Fourteen Points, we asked that the work environment be characterized by:

- Higher employee pride, satisfaction, and involvement.
- A reduction of barriers between working groups.
- A greater focus on facts and problem solving through the use of SPC instead of opinions.
- A leadership dedicated to helping employees satisfy their internal customers.
- A stronger and more cooperative relationship with external suppliers and customers.
- An overall management philosophy of continuous process improvement.

In addition to these guiding principles, it was evident that an ongoing focus for quality improvement was needed. The pursuit of quality—or SPC or "Deming"—was seen by different people in different ways, many times at cross-purposes to one another. Some referred to these new thoughts in a near-religious context, although most preferred to think of it as simply a better way to do business. To one employee, "Deming" meant that all the problems in his area would be solved by management . . . and soon! He was disappointed when this didn't happen.

A Commitment to Quality statement for the division crystallized what was being learned:

> We will become a better and better nickel producing operation by continuously improving the quality of all our processes so that we can provide quality products which are competitive.
>
> Better and better means the continuous improvement in all aspects of our operation including employee pride and satisfaction, quality of products and services, production, productivity and costs, safety and environment, public relations and security of our Division's future.
>
> Quality means the ongoing satisfaction of internal and external customers' needs and expectations.
>
> We will continuously help each other to satisfy our customers.

We will focus on and plan for the future through investment in our people, processes and equipment.

The statement received extensive critiquing, particularly the "better and better" phrase. My preference for "better and better" rather than "best" is based upon its achievability by each individual, each department, and, indeed, the division. This is not to say that the division does not want to be the "best" organization, but that the way to achieve it is by becoming better and better.

This statement has major significance. It challenges the status quo and encourages healthy competition with the past. It promotes greater employee pride and satisfaction as essential for all improvement. It requires the gradual definition, measurement, and improvement of all aspects of division performance. It defines quality as customer satisfaction. It requires supervisory and support personnel to shift their role from primarily directing to that of enhancing the performance of people, their equipment, and their processes.

The reiteration of this Commitment to Quality statement has been fundamental to its growing acceptance. At every opportunity senior management promotes, expects, and focuses on quality principles and SPC, and tries to set personal examples by using these principles. The greater one's knowledge of quality principles—much of which is gained through countless hours of self-study—the more successful their implementation will be in the organization.

Employees must be encouraged to identify their customers, develop operational definitions of product quality characteristics with both their customers and suppliers, and analyze the performance of their processes. For all this to take place, resources must be provided, such as training, and there must be an environment that encourages people to take the first steps to use the new knowledge.

Managers are continually presented with problems, opinions, and suggestions, and decisions are frequently requested in the absence of facts and without the aid of SPC. We disciplined ourselves to ask: What is the *real* cause of an equipment breakdown? Where is the fishbone diagram that shows the possible causes for the breakdown? Where is the checksheet that was used to collect the facts, and what did the stratification of these facts reveal? What possible solutions to the breakdown problems were brainstormed?

In a conventional organization, employees are concerned with satisfying their supervisors. At its worst, supervisors direct and employees do as they are told. The Commitment to Quality statement redirects the focus onto internal suppliers and customers, so that employees satisfy their supervisors by satisfying their customers. This requires redefining the role of the managers, which is the job of the leader, but fulfilling the new role has not been without difficulty. Frustration arose where we knew intellectually how we should act, yet found ourselves (out of years of habit) doing things the old way. Habits of decades are hard to change.

A supervisor's job must go beyond simply directing the workforce to helping employees better serve their customers, and employees must know precisely who their internal customers are and the real purpose of their jobs. For example, a cost analyst's job is not to prepare reports, but to provide accurate, timely, and usable data to allow others to make better decisions. Employees must also know how to measure the quality of their product and how to use SPC for continuous improvement of it. This process (know your customers, identify quality, and measure and improve the product) is continually reinforced, so that it will spread throughout the division.

TQM Coordinators

When the division assumed the responsibility for training, a balance was sought between standardized SPC training across the division and adaptation to local departmental needs. Six people were appointed as TQM Coordinators, each responsible for his or her own departmental SPC training and ongoing support. These Coordinators, valued members of their home departments, with integrity and the ability to help the line organization, are dedicated to seeing SPC work in their own backyards.

Half a year into the program, a Coordinator reporting directly to me was appointed to share the heavy, ongoing load involved in promoting TQM. There were programs to prepare or initiate, speeches to make, literature to review, courses to evaluate, and help to provide to the line organization with implementing TQM and SPC.

We selected a Coordinator with the ability to work with all department heads. He has production experience, and is quick to learn and eager to teach the application of SPC. He is an internal consultant available to all our people, and administers the division aspects of the quality improvement efforts. The Coordinator's office is located near mine for ease of daily consultation. The flow of ideas welling up within the division and from outside demands plenty of discussion and action.

The Coordinator's role is not a substitute for my personal involvement and commitment. The Coordinator is not the head of a quality assurance department or an inspector of quality efforts, but a facilitator whose influence in the drive for quality is based on knowledge and experience, rather than rank. This is viewed as a development position, and these responsibilities are rotated about every three years.

Process Improvement Teams

A key vehicle for improvement is the Process Improvement (PI) Team. Teams are generally divided into natural work groups or crews, or into cross-functional teams with broad expertise. Team members who normally work together are readily able to select problems in their own areas, while the cross-functional teams tend to tackle broader challenges, such as capital projects, cross-divisional issues, and outside supplier selection.

We felt it important not to insist on quick successes, much as these were desired, but to encourage the initially slow and methodical use of SPC tools. Familiarity with these tools did not occur overnight, and it required extra effort until SPC became a comfortable approach to problem solving and process improvement. I vividly recall our waiting for the signal of success in the first years.

Before improvement could be expected, employees had to be educated about quality principles and trained in the use of SPC. Without this, it would have been futile to exhort them to do it right the first time while they were still saddled with incapable processes. Four-week SPC training was given to twenty-five technical personnel, who were expected to teach and apply SPC throughout the division. This was followed by three- to six-day SPC training for employees at all levels. In retrospect, training during the first year was generally too advanced for our beginning needs, and it focused on individual statistical techniques without a coherent model for selecting the appropriate tools in the proper sequence. In some cases, the rate of training exceeded our ability to provide the ongoing support for its application. The importance of team skills was not recognized. This training was eventually simplified, delivered on a just-in-time basis, and focused on the practical use of SPC to improve processes selected by employees.

Teams of varying skills and expertise were established and, as some expressed it, were to go out and "search and destroy." Few were able to. Initial efforts were compromised by a belief that quick results would flow once training was provided. Although knowledge had been partly provided, willingness and opportunity were not always present. We now know there are three elements to success in process improvement: 1) employees must be involved and willing to try new ideas, 2) they must be given the knowledge that allows them to discover better methods, and 3) the work environment must encourage, support, and provide them with the opportunity to do so. In fact, the effectiveness of the teams depends largely on a positive work environment. SPC alone supplies only the tools.

The appointment of TQM Coordinators to provide full-time training and ongoing support in each major department helped address some of these early problems. In addition, a fundamental change involved making supervisors responsible for training and using SPC. Ideally, the trainer trains the supervisor, and the supervisor trains the crew. In practice, the trainer continues to conduct much of the training, but with the active involvement and support of the supervisor. When the supervisor uses and expects the use of SPC on the job, improvement takes place. Without this, progress is minimal.

There were occasions when employee expectations of quick solutions were raised but not fulfilled. We erred by creating the impression that capital would be available if the data indicated the need. Some teams saw this as the ticket to new equipment. It took a year before this failing on our part became evident and, as a result, some teams felt misled and became discouraged. Teams are now encouraged to attempt to improve their processes without falling back on the easy solution of spending a lot of money. This situation is discussed at the start, and much closer contact is maintained with teams throughout their deliberations.

Another aspect of team evolution was that our initial improvement efforts were selected by management and assigned to employees. It became apparent that employees were not as eager to work on someone else's problem as they were on their own. A shift was made to let our people choose the topic for improvement, and this resulted in renewed team activity. Following this, however, it became evident that there were some major initiatives that should be pursued by teams, but which no team had chosen. By assigning volunteers together with people whose jobs involve such studies as part of their normal mandates, a better blend of both is achieved.

Most of us have now learned that no process exists that cannot be improved, but few processes can be improved without using SPC and the QC Story, which guides one in selecting the appropriate SPC tools to use and in what order (Kume 1985). The solutions often appear deceptively simple in retrospect, but they were almost never obvious before using the structured approach of SPC. Although all teams use SPC in some form, not every problem or opportunity requires the full range of tools. Some processes are simple to address, such as the flowcharting of an administrative process to streamline it. Often, simple brainstorming, data collection with a check sheet, and stratifying the main contributors with a Pareto chart are sufficient. Other processes can be more formidable, such as those involving general issues (safety or housekeeping, for example). These may be simplified by reducing the scope of the target, or by simply letting SPC and the QC Story process flush out the fewer, main contributors to be addressed specifically and with priority.

The improvements have been many, varied, and significant. One major challenge we set for the mines was to improve product quality as measured by the grade of ore delivered to the subsequent milling stage. The improvement process involved hundreds of employees at every level in the mine, made up of a long chain of customers and suppliers, from the initial diamond drilling used to locate the ore, to the ore layout plans provided to the production drillers, and to all the subsequent steps through to the mill. The definition of a quality product was determined at each of these stages and, virtually without exception, changes were made to nudge those quality measurements or indicators in the right direction. After one year, savings totalled several million dollars.

There are hundreds of other examples—ranging from improved safety, equipment availability, time needed to perform jobs, housekeeping, final product quality, engineering processes, metal recoveries, effluent quality, energy conservation, supplies quality, and so on. The computer services department is delivering a new and more user-friendly information system based on user-defined requirements, together with technical direction from the services group. Purchasing personnel now view the users of their purchases as their customers, and have shifted their emphasis from initial cost to total cost—again working with users. Although such a step seems obvious, it reflects a marked change in approach and in the system itself.

At present, over two hundred PI Teams are working on production, safety, costs, product quality, administrative processes, and other operating problems and opportunities across the division. It should be emphasized that teams are established when and where they make sense, and that much process improvement comes from people working together who are not organized as formal PI Teams.

The Union

Our experience points strongly to the need to establish an open relationship with the union at the start. Respect for the union's role in TQM may seem automatic, but it must be made clearly evident, and the leader's attitude and approach can help to set the stage for labor-management cooperation. Opportunities for greater constructive union influence are being fostered by joint training, informal meetings, problem solving, and a pursuit of win-win solutions.

Operators, miners, and tradesmen are represented by an industrial union, the United Steelworkers of America. The union executives' initial reaction to the company's intentions about TQM could be characterized as open but neutral. Senior union executives were able to attend Dr. Deming's seminar, and a wait-and-see attitude developed. Over the years, there has been concern about the longer-term benefits to employees as they participated in more activities and achieved greater influence within their work assignments. Some union members are decidedly uncomfortable with increasing employee-company cooperation. Some would like to see the "rules" of total quality better defined, particularly in regard to the union's role.

The relationship with the union has evolved and matured into one of greater respect. Opinions and positions may differ, but through a focus on facts, management and labor are addressing many issues in which both parties have a common interest and a common objective of doing the right thing. A shift has taken place from being preoccupied with incidents to developing processes and systems to handle similar issues that might arise. No doubt there will be serious differences in the future, but we share a growing confidence that they will be addressed constructively.

CONTINUING IMPROVEMENT PLANS

Individual departments are now developing longer-term total quality improvement plans. These plans will provide the framework for achieving the objectives broadly defined in the Commitment to Quality statement. To achieve an objective, one needs a clear understanding of what constitutes quality performance. Exactly what do we want? What is good performance? Are we accomplishing it? How do we measure it, even if only on a subjective scale or by audit? How will we regularly monitor it to ensure that objectives are being met or, if not, to signal a need for higher priority? If process performance is defined, measured, monitored, and continuously improved, better overall results will be achieved.

No organization leader can or would want to monitor all aspects of the organization personally, but it is important to monitor the critical points. This encompasses the plan for how and when measurements will be conducted, by whom, and how they will be reviewed. It constitutes a system for determining when performance is satisfactory or, more importantly, when opportunities indicate a priority effort is needed. This has proved to be more challenging than it first appeared.

Improvement processes usually involve going upstream, often far removed from the desired "bottom line" end result. For example, how does one define good safety performance? Accident frequency rates can be measured, but these are often not a satisfactory measure of performance, particularly in smaller groups. A better measurement might be the status of working conditions and practices that are the real determinants of accidents. Monitoring these situations provides a better indication of performance and focuses on the real contributors to safety.

Similar exercises are needed for production, product quality, and costs. For example, production performance depends on equipment performance and, therefore, equipment availability, mean time between failures, and operating efficiency must be measured and monitored. Cost performance is usually measured by unit cost per pound nickel produced, but by the time this cost is known, it is too late to influence it. Therefore, cost performance is being addressed by focusing on improvement in upstream factors that influence the costs: reagent consumption, explosives efficiencies, labor costs for spillage, unit energy consumption, defective products, and so on.

Mine production is one critical point that determines division performance. Unfortunately, there is considerable natural variation in the ore bodies being mined in terms of size, minability, and grade. To select a measurement of production based solely on pounds nickel is inadequate. After all, the miner has no control over the ore grade as deposited by nature. The miner does, however, have great influence over the way that block of ore is mined, so that dilution with undesirable rock is kept to a minimum and that valuable ore is not left behind. This requires accurate diamond drilling, accurate layouts, accurate production drilling, and so forth. These processes can be measured and, as they are improved, will result in improved division production—and costs. At one time, miners struggled with oversized chunks resulting from the blasting operation. Only after fragmentation was measured and monitored as "chunks per 1,000 tons," was improvement made possible through new drill patterns—which affected not only production, but costs and safety as well.

PROMOTING IMPROVEMENT

Personal Appeals

The organization leader must persist in making clear a strong expectation of continuing process improvement in every aspect of the organization. During the first year, personal appeals to employees were made to participate in the pursuit of quality: safer working conditions, better quality materials for processing, reduced costs, and better job security and working conditions. In addition, we suggested there would be far greater opportunity for growth, participation, contribution, and influence within the division.

The first formal appeals were made at employee communication sessions given once or twice a year to all two thousand employees in small groups. These sessions, which have been held for many years, typically deal with the health of the world nickel industry, Inco's financial situation, division performance, and issues of topical interest.

These initial appeals, based on a vision, carried only so much weight, but they nurtured the openness to change. Many strong-minded individuals debated openly the perceived adoption of Japanese management techniques in the North American culture. Who was Dr. Deming, anyway? There was also healthy skepticism that this was simply another management program that would come and go. Employees needed to see evidence of management's sincerity and interest in helping them do their jobs and building pride and satisfaction in their work.

We have learned over and over that we must reinforce the concepts of quality at every opportunity—at all meetings and discussions. Skepticism has gradually evolved into acceptance and active participation in the new way of doing business. Many of those who were the most vociferous five years ago are, today, the strongest TQM advocates and practitioners.

Newsletter

A "Quality Update" column was established in the biweekly employee newsletter to promote and acknowledge quality improvement. This column has been superseded by a steady flow of articles that describe people improving their processes. Employees are urged to submit their stories, and rather than focusing on results, the articles stress the principles and methods people are using to approach a problem or an opportunity.

The newsletter is an important vehicle for acknowledging employee initiatives and disseminating knowledge of quality. It is not a glossy publication, nor is it intended to win public affairs awards. It is intended to give its customers the information they request, as determined by employee surveys every two years. The newsletter is now published weekly and has tripled in size. Senior management studies each article before publication to ensure that the principles of quality are highlighted and that the effort of employees is recognized more so than the results.

QUIP Meetings

Department heads attend biweekly Quality Improvement Progress (QUIP) meetings as a forum for promoting and sharing experiences. Participants give six ten-minute reviews on topics that demonstrate how SPC or quality methods have been effective and how they might be used in other areas. QUIP meetings have helped create greater cooperation between departments. These meetings have given me an opportunity to express support and encouragement and to emphasize how each demonstrates quality principles or the use of SPC.

QUIP meetings are also held within each department to acknowledge and encourage team progress. These provide visible evidence of management's interest and involvement within the department. These regular reports to management set the pulse for improvement. QUIP meetings at both the department and division levels include team presentations, which are celebrated. They provide an outstanding opportunity to acknowledge contributions.

SUMMARY

The Cost of Quality

Organizations must improve their processes to remain viable. As quality principles permeate all aspects of a business, the apparent cost of quality—that is, for training, for meeting times, for benchmarking, for gathering additional data—will become accepted as a normal cost of doing business. It would be short-sighted to isolate the costs of pursuing quality, just as it would be to focus on the costs of pursuing safety. The cost of non-quality is substantial and probably much more than assumed. My experience is that opportunities for improvement are unlimited.

Management as a Process

An initial perception was that the pursuit of quality is a supplementary activity added to the normal managerial functions of planning, organizing, leading, and controlling. This is true, to the extent that the new principles and SPC tools do require additional effort. As we turn our attention to the subjects of production, costs, safety, and so on, quality principles and SPC now enter into virtually every aspect of our thinking. Management itself is a process and it, too, has been improved.

Managers throughout the organization are expected to use quality principles and SPC to improve processes within their responsibilities. People who do not use the quality principles lack either the knowledge, the skill, or the opportunity to do so. Those who are ineffective need help in acquiring these skills. We try to move quickly to provide the needed resources and personal support and involvement.

One-on-one discussions with managers and general advice on how to approach an issue can be helpful. Often, thoughtful questions based on statistical thinking are sufficient, such as: What are the quality characteristics of your department's products and processes? What possible causes of poor quality have been suggested by brainstorming? What facts did the check sheets and Pareto charts reveal, and what is their order of importance? What are the brainstormed possible solutions to these problems or opportunities? We persistently encourage managers to solve their problems through teamwork and fact-based management.

A Change in Attitude

The transformation of an organization begins with the transformation of its leadership. Most of us in leadership positions have always thought of our own enlightenment, yet a change in attitude takes place. This change is one of intensity, not a total redirection. In fact, one might choose to view quality principles and SPC as a method for sharing what one has always believed. After all, who has ever been opposed to quality and problem solving and respect for employees? To the extent that attitudes are shaped by increased knowledge and the successful experience of using quality principles, the organization leader becomes even more enthusiastic and demanding. Attitude, knowledge, and effectiveness are enhanced synergistically.

To say that our operation has become dedicated and effective in pursuing quality in all endeavors would be premature. Although progress has been made on all fronts, substantial opportunity for improvement remains. My job remains to ensure that through the unrelenting pursuit of quality as a philosophy, continuous improvement is achieved in order that the enterprise can sell its products and services to an increasingly demanding market.

2

The Executive Steering Committee

A. WAYNE STEWART, ET AL.
Dominion Bridge

The Executive Steering Committee is composed of senior management from each of the organization's major functional areas and, where appropriate, elected union leadership (Figure 2.1). Ideally, the Committee should have no more than twelve members, including the CEO and the TQM Coordinator.

The Committee's primary purpose is to plan, implement, check, and ensure that the necessary steps are being taken to develop a TQM organization.

The Committee's major responsibilities are to:

- Establish and lead the transformation effort.
- Work towards the organizational mission.
- Establish priorities and critical objectives.
- Plan for continuous improvement with all customers and suppliers.
- Support learning in the organization.
- Create an atmosphere for cultural change.
- Model all phases of the effort.

This chapter describes the efforts of the Executive Steering Committee at Dominion Bridge.

19

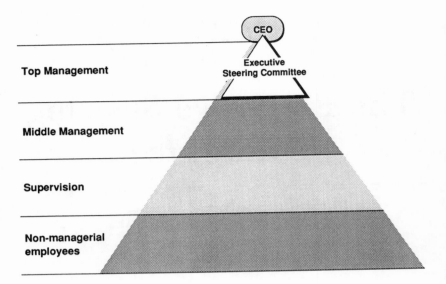

FIGURE 2.1

PROFILE: DOMINION BRIDGE, WESTERN CANADA

The Western Canada Structural Division of Dominion Bridge, a United Dominion Company, is based in Winnipeg, Manitoba, and operates four basic businesses: structural steel fabrication, special hardware products, reinforcing steel products, and a Steel Service Center. Our 500 employees include 140 salaried employees and 360 unionized production workers. Our manufacturing space totals 275,000 square feet in two plants.

The steel markets rapidly fell to fifty percent of their prior levels in the early 1980s in Western Canada. This was an industry crisis accompanied by significant red ink. Plant closures, long-term lay-offs, and headcount reductions became the norm, and our corporation permanently closed three of its five plants in Western Canada. As the shakeout and market stabilized, we realized we needed something different if we were to rise from the proverbial ashes. Investing in technology alone would not do it. We prepared for long-term quality improvement.

We had used both restructuring and investment in new technology throughout this crisis, but neither approach yielded the results we anticipated. Our search began for another approach, one that would give the workers a personal stake in the company. In other words, we started from the viewpoint that the workers just weren't giving the company enough effort. We couldn't give them shares in the company, so we looked at various incentive schemes. Although incentives could buy short-term interest, we concluded, they didn't answer the question of once interested, what do you do next? We knew training was part of the answer, but what training?

We had a long history of excellence in engineering design, fabrication, and construction. We could build a project on time and on budget. We had a history of effective control. But control was not what we needed; we needed change.

The company did not have a systematic process to improve the things we were doing, and the principles and practices of TQM appeared to answer our problems. Simply stated, these were: the right environment, empowering our employees, continuous improvement, a systematic application of tools and techniques, the concept of process and improvement coming from those who work in the process, and the overall goal of meeting or exceeding customer expectations, both external and internal.

Now all that remained was to make these become our way of life.

THE STEERING COMMITTEE'S LEADERSHIP ROLE

The Executive Steering Committee is the element that lends leadership to the transformation process. Leadership is essential if TQM is to become a living part of the organization and sensitized to our values and principles. From the first day, we recognized that this was not a process we would complete in a short time.

We brainstormed the objectives that define our leadership role:

- Understand the process and the new underlying philosophy in the language of our industry. Acquire knowledge.
- Champion the task ahead, and provide the leadership and motivation for our staff to follow the process.
- Set our unit's vision and deploy it to the organization.
- Act as role models. Improve our own personal processes, and

encourage, empower, and support others in their efforts to do the same.
- Plan the implementation process, and check progress and effectiveness as we go forward.
- Provide training at the appropriate time.
- Act as a resource to support the acquisition of knowledge by others.
- Allocate the resources needed both to serve current customers and to move toward our goals.
- Schedule, control, and teach the consultants to talk our language.
- Revise policies and practices to support the transition to our goals.

We decided that the Committee would parallel our existing management structure. The CEO and all his direct reports formed the Committee, and we appointed the human resources manager as the meeting facilitator/coordinator. This structure gave us two immediate advantages: we were already functioning as a team, and we were, under all management definitions, ultimately responsible for optimizing the company's performance and delivering an acceptable product to our customers.

Union leadership was not included on the Committee, because their role as politicians places them in circumstances that are difficult and more variable than management's. Later, we tried to include them in our first round of training, and they appeared genuinely open to the initiative. Unfortunately, they were viewed as being "in management's pocket" and were defeated in subsequent union elections. We concluded our best path was to deal with our employees and that their politicians would follow.

Because the company was still in an industry crisis, we did not want to chance delegating to others what we viewed as our strategy for survival. We also wanted to ensure that, as TQM became the way of life at Dominion Bridge, it became the way of life of its leadership first. Communication became a key issue for us at this point and throughout the transformation process. The company did not have a history of open communication. It was not so much that we were closed and secret, but we had the typical hierarchy in which management made decisions: we were not accustomed to explaining ourselves down, only up, in the organization. If the principles of TQM were to succeed, it was clear this had to change.

Setting expectations too soon, however, would increase the risk of failure or, at best, make the task more difficult. We concluded that general correspondence to the majority of our employees would be kept to a minimum. The Executive Committee had to be prepared with a consistent philosophy and consistent answers. We would need to explain management's "other pressures" that might stop us from taking action on proposed changes. And our employees would need time to learn.

OUR FIRST STEPS

We deliberately set the mechanics of the Executive Committee to be different from normal. We established a formal team process for our meetings: appointing a facilitator, preparing an agenda, recording our progress, and working toward the goal of consensus decision making with everyone's active participation. Also, our weekly two-hour meetings began thirty minutes ahead of regular office hours, since we recognized the transition was going to take extra effort. We wanted to role-model the extra effort required and, from a practical standpoint, give ourselves a longer day.

Acquiring a working knowledge of the new management principles was our first task. Half of the management team had attended a four-day Deming seminar in the previous quarter, and we now hired external consultants to put on a three-day seminar for the Committee and the majority of our supervisors and other key personnel. This need to acquire knowledge, by the way, is ongoing. Committee members should set up a reading program, attend quality seminars and ASQC meetings, and establish a network with counterparts in other organizations involved in TQM.

The Committee spent the next fourteen weeks studying Deming's Fourteen Points, concentrating on one point each week. We looked at their significance and benefit to the organization and our people, and at examples of following and not following the principles. It was clear that we differed in accepting these new principles and in understanding how they would yield bottom-line improvements. This should have come as no surprise, but we found that acceptance and buy-in grew as we progressed.

In our fifth month, we started working on our branch vision and operating philosophy to align the company's aims and purposes with those of TQM. Our vision for the company was that we would be:

- The premier supplier of steel-related services or products.
- Dominant in the markets or market segments served.
- Respected in our community.
- Emulated by our competitors.
- Known as *the* place to work.
- Sought after by our customers.
- Focused on improving all things that we do.
- Meeting and exceeding our customers' expectations.
- Earning consistent profitability.
- Providing cash for returns to the shareholders, as well as investment in equipment and people.

This vision statement was translated into an operating philosophy based on constantly striving to be the best, never-ending improvement, recognizing the needs of our employees, customers, shareholders, suppliers, and government, and on having people with a commitment to teamwork, education, and training.

Our next step was to set up the education and training program for the organization. Our original consulting plan called for our external consultants, one behavioral and one statistical, to act as facilitators, supporting us two or three days per month. Our SPC training started with the Executive Committee. Three days of classroom training were followed by three weeks off, during which every participant worked on a project by applying and becoming comfortable with the new tools. This was followed by three more days of training.

Just as there is variance in every process, there was variance in the response and acceptance of applying SPC tools to the projects selected by the Committee members. At this point, learning to use the tools on a project selected for that purpose was still mostly regarded as time-consuming and extra work. We eventually attained our objective, developing an awareness of the importance of using these tools.

One of the projects we selected involved our cash flow forecasting, which we had been trying to improve for some time and generally thought of as showing good progress. We established a systematic review of all accounts versus our progress on product delivery to establish our collections forecast. When we used the tools and collected the data, however, we could see that, in fact, there had been no improvement at all. Collections seemed to be consistently falling short of the forecast by $100,000. When presented with the data, our controller admitted he felt the collection targets were not aggressive enough, and so he had been adding $100,000 each month. No wonder we didn't reach our collection goal! This taught us the importance of involving the people who actually work in the process, and that the tools are not only useful but can actually reveal counterproductive behavior by management.

We also needed to start SPC training for our in-house specialists, who were sent on a course for one week each month over a three-month period. These specialists, who would become our facilitators in SPC techniques, were selected from a variety of backgrounds to represent our different businesses. Two were from the Executive Committee: the reinforcing-steel product manager and the manager of engineering. The others were the estimating supervisor, production supervisor, project supervisor, and the shipping foreman. SPC training was then to follow throughout the organization and be completed in six months. We saw the education of the philosophy cascading through the organization and believed we would then be ready to start improving processes.

Parallel with the statistical training, we established two Quality Leadership Teams, which we called Quality Management Improvement Teams (QMITs), to study improvements in the work environment. We divided the Fourteen Points into two general groups: principles and practices. The QMITs were given the mandate to acquire knowledge, study the principles, review our interpretation of those principles, and then start to identify barriers to their implementation. We let them work out their own mechanics and pick the priorities as they saw them. For example, one QMIT chose to look at the principle of instituting leadership (point 7) and identified barriers such as the lack of understanding one's day-to-day job functions and the lack of a network for communication. Looking at the principle of driving out fear (point 8), they identified "fear of the boss" as well as fear caused by not knowing what is expected. Each member of the Executive Committee became the champion of at least one principle and acted as the liaison with the QMIT.

Our plan also called for establishing a Local Steering Committee in each functional area: At first, we questioned the need for another set of committees and more meetings, but the Executive Committee alone cannot coordinate all the projects as they multiply throughout the organization. The Executive Committee must continue to support these projects by establishing clear priorities, empowering the team members, and encouraging and monitoring their progress, but Local Steering Committees are imperative to coordinate the process improvement efforts in each area.

CRISIS

At the end of our first fourteen weeks, we had reached a crisis. We had finished our study of the Fourteen Points and developed our mission, we had QMITs going, we had seventy-five people trained in the philosophy and thirty trained in SPC tools. But conflict was mounting, and there was no clear path forward. There were a number of factors behind this crisis:

- We had started by using the consultants' plan without taking time to personalize it. In fact, we did not really hear the plan—we only wanted to know what to do next.
- Our management group had not attended the Deming seminar together. If we had done so, it would have helped bind us through the shared experience and reduce the need for half the team to play catch-up with the other half.
- Our statistical consulting and training started too soon, resulting in a delay before we started using the tools. Knowledge, interest, and enthusiasm were lost.
- We had trained too many people too fast. We should not have trained past our management group at first, so that we could have had time to learn more before starting others in the process. Too many projects were undertaken, and without proper leadership and the resources to support them, the teams were in conflict and the projects were faltering.
- We thought that people could pick a project or process by themselves. We had held back giving direction because we thought it would be interpreted as interfering in their self-management.
- We should have provided more specific leadership to the QMITs, and waited six to nine months into the transformation before starting them. We wanted them to be free from the autocratic

direction of management, but they wanted to work in areas and on issues that we were not ready, willing, or able to deal with. This created some friction with both the Executive and Local Steering Committees, particularly on sensitive issues, and also resulted in wasted effort as we worked parallel to each other.

One QMIT, for example, was working on the issue of the lack of understanding one's day-to-day job functions while the Executive Committee was trying to sort out a process to determine what critical functions should be. We just were not prepared to deal with their recommendation at that time. They were frustrated that their recommendations were not implemented, and we were disturbed that they were working in parallel.

Another QMIT was studying point 5, the continual improvement of the system for production and service. One of the barriers to this point was our inconsistent workload, which resulted in alternately expanding our short-term capacity through overtime and then cutting our capacity through temporary layoffs. This, of course, can cause a number of problems: low morale, equipment ruin, lack of skills development, and process variability. The QMIT recommended that we establish a core level of employees with no layoffs, and that sales and marketing be geared to sell to that level. The Executive Committee's fear, however, was that committing to no layoffs would increase the possibility of substantial losses, and that an increased selling effort would raise costs with no assurance of increased business. Their impatience to find a solution quickly was in conflict with our long-term strategy to improve processes, differentiate through quality, and achieve the lowest total cost, which eventually would give us the ability to attract a more consistent workload.

We attempted to ease this friction by refocusing QMITs to be a resource to the line organization. QMITs were eventually disbanded, because their focus became similar to what we wanted from the Local Steering Committee: that local areas should resolve their own concerns.

"WHAT MATTERS"

Working on the Fourteen Points had given us a structured process for teamwork and consensus decision making, and we were developing good habits. However, we had reached the point where we were trained but had lost confidence in what to do next. We needed a focus and a "why" for establishing teams. We needed to identify our expectations from the top down and decide where to invest the time and resources for improvement.

We decided to slow down and first improve our own critical processes. We tried to define the most important processes with which each member of the Executive Steering Committee dealt. This was frustrating and time-consuming. It was difficult to maintain a clear focus, because we were mixing our individual day-to-day duties with the functional responsibilities of running our various businesses and with what our external customers seemed to expect. Eventually, we uncomplicated the process by simply establishing "what matters" to each of our customers.

In two of our businesses, we used customer surveys to determine their expectations and how we could meet their needs. One survey concentrated on customers for which our market share was low. This mail-out survey was followed up with phone calls and interviews to make sure we understood the data. The other survey started with our top twenty accounts. In addition to a standard list of quality and service attributes, we asked how we compared to our competitors. To reduce bias, we then selected ten accounts where the customers did not award us with the majority of their business. The results of the ten accounts did not differ appreciably from that of the twenty.

After we gained this perspective of both internal and external customers, we identified processes in which the Committee members already worked or for which they were responsible. Opinions differed about starting with easy or difficult problems and processes, but we decided to choose those that were critical to the ongoing success of our business. These critical processes were in our individual annual business plans, involving areas such as process control versus inspection, training and education, and internalizing our vision. The whole management group brainstormed the processes, and then used weighted voting to purge out the less important. In this way, management from a variety of disciplines was able to contribute their own particular viewpoint to the formation of these processes in all of our businesses. Then we set out, as individuals, to improve them.

Our "what matters" approach provided a convenient way to discuss the process and provide leadership and direction to our improvement initiatives. Management grew comfortable using the new tools, which became evident in our daily problem solving. No meeting was complete without a white board and a brainstorming session.

EPILOGUE

Although many people characterized TQM as putting all the people to work on their processes, we found that they in fact needed more leadership and direction than ever before. To help provide this leadership, the Executive Steering Committee must work on the company's overall vision, so that every level of the organization can understand and buy into it. Only then will improvement efforts be mutually supportive and pull in the same direction.

After two years into the transformation process, we see the Committee as a mixed process—part management process improvements, and part transformation to a new philosophy. As our awareness and knowledge grew, so did our role. We are convinced that having the full management team function as the Executive Committee is the best approach. The Committee has begun to take on many basic management functions, and eventually the role of the Committee will blend with the role of management.

3

The Local Steering Committee

LAWRENCE A. LUCCHESI
Chevron Chemical Company

The Local Steering Committee is composed of a senior area manager (who should also be a member of the Executive Steering Committee) and the manager's immediate staff (Figure 3.1). Union leadership should also be included where appropriate. The Committee works to establish the improvement effort in a particular business unit. An organization may have several Local Steering Committees, depending on its size and geographical dispersion.

The Committee works under the guidance of the Executive Steering Committee to implement a continuous improvement plan for all processes directly related to major priorities in the corporate mission or plan.

The Local Steering Committee's major responsibilities are to:

- Identify and monitor critical processes, quality measures, and customer requirements.
- Establish and champion process improvement efforts.
- Commission and support Process Improvement (PI) Teams.
- Provide process improvement skills for employees.
- Keep all employees informed and work with other Local Steering Committees to coordinate the overall effort.

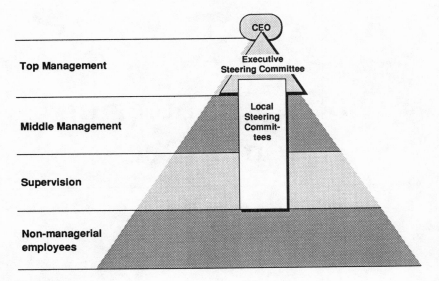

FIGURE 3.1

- Provide for recognition of improvement efforts and achievements.
- Identify local areas and opportunities for culture change efforts.

This chapter describes the efforts of the Local Steering Committee at Chevron Chemical Company.

PROFILE: CHEVRON CHEMICAL COMPANY, OLEFINS AND DERIVATIVES DIVISION

Our Cedar Bayou plant manufactures basic petrochemicals and their derivatives, including thermoplastic resins. It is one of several manufacturing plants in the Olefins Division of Chevron Chemical Company, which has a total of six divisions in diversified segments of the chemical business.

The plant provides nine hundred full-time jobs, including over three hundred contractor employees in mechanical maintenance and product packaging. One maintenance contractor has enjoyed a long-term single-source relationship with the plant, and turnover in this group has been low. There are about four hundred hourly and non-exempt employees, including process operators, instrument, electrical and lab technicians, and clerical and stores employees. There are about fifty-five first-line supervisors in the field, the majority being operating shift supervisors. The entire plant workforce is nonunion.

OUR CHARTER AND INITIAL EFFORTS

Our quality improvement program was initiated at the division level, and represented the first commitment to such a program anywhere in the corporation. The impetus for this program came from our customers. Most of them were satisfied with our product quality, but they were beginning to require their suppliers to show some evidence of a quality program and commitment to continuous improvement. Our divisional management studied the quality principles and techniques of several leading authorities, and decided to proceed based on Deming's philosophy. This commitment by the division's vice president and general manager firmly set the stage for participation by the entire division.

We decided to use an external consultant at the very outset, realizing we didn't have the "profound knowledge" of which Deming speaks. An Executive Steering Committee (which we called a Division Steering Committee) was formed with the general manager as chairman, and consisting of the division's functional managers and plant managers. With the help of our consultant, the Committee worked for four months to develop an organizational structure for the quality improvement program, patterned after the consultant's model. This plan included three Quality Leadership Teams to study the Fourteen Points, and called for the formation of a Local Steering Committee at each of the division's separate locations to steer their individual improvement efforts.

Membership

Our Local Steering Committee is chaired by the plant manager and includes managers of the various plant functions, the superintendent of quality control labs, and the plant statisticians. The Committee normally meets once a month, and we schedule special meetings to hear team presentations on completed process improvement projects. During the first year, one of the external consultants also participated as a full member of the Committee to keep us on track, particularly in regard to applying the Fourteen Points to our efforts. The consultant's role with the Committee later changed from full membership to being available for spot consultation as needed.

Our original intent was to include only one plant statistician on the Committee, but we decided to include four engineers who had been trained in advanced statistics. This base of statistical knowledge helped us get started with finding suitable SPC applications in the plant. Their knowledge proved invaluable, and a group of statisticians now holds permanent membership in the Committee. Our statisticians, who are all exempt employees with full-time jobs in the plant in addition to their process improvement roles, are selected and trained only after they express interest in the opportunity and the willingness to take on the extra time and effort. They have been outstanding champions of the new philosophy and indispensable catalysts for continuing the program.

Mission and Objectives

We decided that our mission as a Local Steering Committee was to:

- Implement the Quality Leadership Teams' recommendations for removing our organizational barriers to the Fourteen Points.
- Develop and implement in-house SPC applications.

Our main objectives were to:

- Provide visible and continuous management support for the overall quality improvement program.
- Make sure that all employees are trained in the Fourteen Points and statistics.
- Provide a formal team structure for involving all employees in the program.

The Quality Leadership Teams identified many organizational barriers to the Fourteen Points, most of them stemming from a history of authoritarian culture in which management made most decisions without first consulting the people who would be affected.

On a number of occasions, we invited the Quality Leadership Teams to our meetings to update us on special projects they were working on, such as single-sourcing and customer-supplier awareness. This has helped us enhance our employees' involvement in the program.

In retrospect, implementing the Quality Leadership Teams' recommendations has probably occupied less than twenty percent of our time. And a funny thing happened on the way: it took us a year or so to realize that we alone could not cause SPC to be implemented and accepted plant-wide. A few applications were indeed identified and accepted at the outset, but SPC did not spread rapidly as we had hoped. In hindsight, the reasons are very clear: we had not yet provided our employees and supervisors with sufficient knowledge of the statistical tools or with a process for putting them to use.

Training

During the first several months of our work, we needed to start some initial improvement projects while simultaneously guiding the necessary education and training in the Fourteen Points and SPC. The training would give us some idea of what we were trying to accomplish, and the actual use of SPC would give the entire workforce a common language to use in problem solving. The training, which was mandatory for all employees, was a sizable and concentrated effort.

Supervisory and Technical Employees

During the first five months of the program, the plant's supervisory and technical personnel—about 120 employees—attended our consultant's introductory course in quality improvement. As this training neared completion, we began putting the same group through statistical training covering the use of basic tools such as Pareto charts, fishbone diagrams, tally sheets, histograms, control charts, and standard deviation. This course was a major effort, requiring three days in each of two separate weeks. Our plant statisticians were the instructors, and the technical personnel who attended the earlier classes served as additional instructors later on. This training took about six months to complete.

Hourly Employees

In our third month, we appointed a task force of one statistician and two operating area superintendents to prepare statistical training for the hourly and nonexempt personnel in our plant—more than three hundred people. The three-day course included a session on the Fourteen Points and was tailored as much as possible to actual plant examples. Technical personnel and first-line supervisors were co-instructors for these classes, with our statisticians available as consultants.

After several months of course preparation and instructor training, the classes began and ran continuously for four months, during which 311 employees were trained. Each class was visited by one or two of the plant management staff to explain the organizational structure of the quality improvement program, and to talk with them about the Fourteen Points.

Employees were frequently concerned that this program was another fad that lacked the commitment of top management. Several years previously, for example, we had embraced a concept of productivity based simply on the ratio of output to input, such as pounds of production per hours worked. We had defined and tracked a number of "productivity" parameters, but they were largely meaningless to the workforce, because we had no *process* for improving them. So employees now correctly pointed out that while the Fourteen Points sounded good, it was management's job to see them implemented. We clearly had our work cut out for us.

Contractors

All company personnel had now received initial training, and we decided it would be appropriate to train at least the supervisory group of our contract workforce. Our maintenance contractor had earlier adopted its own version of a quality improvement program but had not provided statistical training for employees. Plant and contractor management compared notes on training and philosophy, and agreed that the differences were not significant in many respects. The contractor agreed that we should provide statistical training for its supervisors. Our plant statisticians accomplished this over the next several months, again tailoring standard course material to their actual maintenance activities.

The First Year

We spent most of the first year attempting to foster SPC projects that the Local Steering Committee itself originated, or that surfaced through the statistical training exercises for supervisors. We hoped to achieve a few early successes so that the use of SPC techniques would spread rapidly, spawn more projects, and involve more people throughout the plant.

Within the first two months, the Committee selected six projects that included all major plant process areas, and which represented problems or opportunities with the possibility of quick success. Individual statisticians were assigned to each project to investigate the feasibility of collecting accurate data and to encourage project sponsorship by various operating or maintenance groups. Of these six early projects, only two eventually met with tangible success.

Six months into the program, we had a total of twenty projects with groups of two to seven supervisory/technical people working on each one. Nine projects were in the area of operations, seven in maintenance, two in joint operations/maintenance areas, and two in accounting. At this time, the Committee members were assigned to facilitate projects in their areas, and to provide the resources needed by the project groups.

At the ten-month mark, a review showed three projects successfully completed and seven actively working, but five were floundering and five had been cancelled. A number of these projects were not attracting the interest and support of field personnel, and we began to realize that these were top–down projects conceived by management: employees had no feeling of ownership. We needed to get supervisors and employees directly involved in the program, and we needed to provide a formal team structure to support the process.

INVOLVING SUPERVISORS

We had now been more than one year into the program at the plant level. Basic training of all employees was complete. A number of SPC projects were in progress throughout the plant, and a few had been notable successes. But we were well aware that few hourly employees were actively involved in the program. Training had heightened their expectations, but there was no formal structure for their involvement.

It seemed that our first-line supervisors should be playing a key part in the program, but in general were not. To encourage their increased participation, we decided to hold a special one-day offsite meeting for all plant supervisors. Over a two-month period we developed an agenda and engaged speakers.

The meeting focused on management's responsibility, including all levels of supervision, to get on with the transformation. We emphasized situational leadership and the coaching role of the supervisor. These presentations were followed by group brainstorming sessions facilitated by a company trainer, one of our external consultants, and our plant statisticians. The sessions aimed at identifying supervisors' perceptions of barriers to implementing the new philosophy.

This meeting was well received by supervisors, but when it was over they had unloaded some seventy-two barriers onto the Committee's lap! As a follow-up, we appointed a small focus group of six first-line supervisors and three middle-management personnel to consolidate and prioritize the concerns.

Improving Communications. The foremost concern was the need for improved communications. The Committee responded by making wider distribution of its meeting minutes and by instituting, for the first time in the plant's history, the recording and plant-wide distribution of our weekly management staff meetings. Reaction from employees and supervisors alike proved extremely favorable.

Reviewing Policies. Another significant outcome was the formation of a policy review committee chaired by the human resources manager and consisting of second-line supervisors and superintendents from all operating areas. This committee continues to review and update personnel policies, and has improved the uniformity of policy administration throughout the plant. Regular quarterly meetings are now held by the human resources manager with all first-line supervisors to review and clarify policy matters.

Coordinating Training. A third area over which supervisors had voiced major concern was the need for more training. This surprised us in view of the recent concentrated training in quality and statistics. What supervisors wanted, however, was more leadership training for themselves and more skills training for their employees. These concerns led to developing a training course for team leaders, and creating a new position of plant training coordinator. This is a superintendent-level position in the human resources department that now holds a permanent seat on the Local Steering Committee.

Even though training in our plant and our division is still considered a responsibility of line management, the tremendous upsurge in training and retraining of all kinds (quality, statistics, supervisory skills, employee skills, safety, environmental, hazardous materials, and so on) makes overall training coordination a much-needed function.

DEVELOPING EMPLOYEE QUALITY TEAMS

The stage was now set for getting all plant employees involved in the quality improvement program. The need to establish a formal structure for our Quality Teams (PI Teams) had been the subject of discussion as early as six months into our program, but, as mentioned, there had been detours along the way. The major points the Committee considered about PI/Quality Teams were:

- How should they be organized?
- What would they be asked to do?
- How should they be given management support?
- How should they be recognized for achievement?

Team Members

We decided that Quality Teams should parallel the formal plant organization, in order to involve all levels of supervision. We also felt that natural work teams would be the most effective, made up of those employees who regularly worked together.

We formed teams of operators from the four shifts in each of the eight process units, two analyst teams from each of the laboratories, five instrument and electrical teams based on assigned areas of coverage, plus teams in various service groups such as purchasing, central stores, safety/medical, accounting, and secretarial. This resulted in fifty teams that included all hourly and nonexempt employees in the plant.

The regular supervisor of each work group was designated the team leader. For example, the shift supervisors of the operating groups also became the Quality Team leaders. This departmental structure was generally successful. We have formed some cross-functional teams to address specific issues beyond the scope of a natural work team, and we expect to see more of these in the future.

Project Criteria

Teams were asked to select projects that met one of three criteria:

1. Improve the quality of products and services that go to internal and external customers. Quality means consistently meeting the needs of the customer. Reducing variability and truly satisfying customer requirements are the goals.
2. Improve the productivity of existing work processes. Improving productivity means working and communicating more efficiently.
3. Improve profitability by undertaking projects that will reduce costs or provide a reasonable benefit.

A fourth criterion, that of improving safety, was later added at the request of a number of our employees.

Statistical Support

To support the teams in the use of statistics, each team was assigned an advisor from our group of seven statisticians. The advisors consult with the teams about data collection, analysis, and presentation. They are not spokespersons at presentations, nor do they function as team leaders.

This was a big help in getting teams to move ahead on their projects, but it immediately created another problem: with only seven plant statisticians, each had seven to ten teams to advise. Because of shift schedules, the Quality Teams' monthly meetings had to be conducted after hours, thus adding even greater demands on our statisticians' time. This prompted us to train more statisticians. We now have twelve statisticians at the plant and plan to increase the number to sixteen within a year.

Review Committees

We developed a formal problem-solving process within which Quality Teams were asked to work. An important feature is that each group of teams has a review committee that decides whether a Quality Team's proposal meets the criteria for project work, and whether the supporting data is appropriate and properly presented.

Review committees have three members: the department's second-line supervisor, a superintendent or manager, and a neutral technical supervisor from outside the department. This structure is intended to involve middle management in the process, and to make it possible for project implementation to be handled at the lowest possible level of authority for approvals and expenditures.

Customer/Supplier Exercise

Initial group meetings with team leaders acquainted them with the formal team process. The teams were then asked to use their first meetings to work through a structured customer-supplier exercise, which had been developed by one of the Quality Leadership Teams and piloted by one of our plant groups. This exercise was meant to help them select projects by having them identify and interview their customers and suppliers, most of whom are internal. Within three months, most teams had completed the customer-supplier exercise and developed a preliminary list of projects to consider.

The results of this exercise were mixed, however, and we have never successfully repeated it. This was primarily due to a lack of uniform team effort. Some teams worked on it harder than others; some actually interviewed their customers while others did not. Also, service groups such as the maintenance group could clearly see that operations personnel were their customers; but an operator's work product is a chemical that is sent to a remote and rarely seen customer. Since the great majority of our personnel are operators, this exercise was less meaningful to them.

Technical Quality Teams

At this time the Committee examined how the Quality Team process could include our technical staff, most of whom are engineers in the maintenance and engineering departments. All these employees were invited to a brainstorming session facilitated by the consultant. The group identified a number of issues for Quality Team projects and formed eight cross-functional teams, with a number of employees volunteering for two or more teams. These Technical Quality Teams selected their own leaders and scribes, developed mission statements, and began work on their projects.

Team Leadership Training

Although our PI/Quality Teams were making progress, it was slow going, and it became evident after several months that the team leaders needed more in-depth training. This had also been pointed out earlier by our supervisors. Most of the team leaders were supervisors of their work groups, and they had been selected as supervisors primarily because of their operating skills. Leading a team, however, demanded a degree of facilitative skills that they lacked.

Our divisional coordinator worked with the various local training coordinators to develop a team leadership training course. This is a three-day course that covers leadership, meeting mechanics, interpersonal skills, and group dynamics. Over a five-month period, more than seventy plant personnel attended this course, including all team leaders and some second-line supervisors.

While this training was very helpful, it wasn't a panacea. We have since allowed teams to select their own leader, who may be a peer rather than a supervisor. In these cases, the new leader goes through team leadership training, and the supervisor is expected to assume the role of team coach.

Monitoring and Recognizing Progress

About five months after establishing the Quality Team structure for hourly employees, six teams had been through the review committee step. Another five months elapsed before the first team project was presented to the Local Steering Committee. During this time, we developed a quarterly reporting system to monitor the progress of all teams. Reporting was initially handled by the plant statisticians in their role as team advisors, but has since been turned over to line management to strengthen their participation in the program.

We also developed a plan for recognizing Quality Teams that complete a project by having them make a final presentation to the Local Steering Committee. These twenty-minute presentations are introduced by the team leaders, but are given by one or more of the team members themselves. We videotape each presentation, including the follow-up discussion between the Committee and team members. Videotaping preserves the presentation for posterity and for future use by any interested parties. Also, the prospect of going "on camera" usually means the team will organize and prepare its presentation thoroughly.

Recognition for completed projects includes four elements:

1. A plant-wide bulletin board posting that briefly describes the project and its benefits to the plant, and lists all participating team members.
2. Special hard hat stickers for the team members recognizing them as Leaders in Quality.
3. A letter of commendation to each team member from the plant manager, with a copy placed in the employee's personnel file.
4. A cake-and-ice-cream party given by the team's departmental management, and held at their regular work location. Local Steering Committee members are also invited.

These forms of recognition and publicity can motivate and encourage teams to pursue their projects to completion, and they seem to be well received by our employees. In addition, we are now piloting a recognition and awards program that makes monetary awards available to teams or individuals for outstanding achievement. This is a division-wide program in which any team or individual can nominate another. A divisional committee evaluates the nominated achievements, which are many and varied, but quality projects are given a high priority in this program.

Budgeting

A total of seventeen projects, involving ten separate areas or departments of the plant, were presented to the Local Steering Committee over a seven-month period. About half of these projects required capital appropriations, while others merely involved procedural changes with little or no cost to implement them. As the capital projects began to go through the review committee, we were able to accommodate most of them by adjusting the plant's capital budget in advance. No specific funds had been pre-budgeted for Quality Team projects during the first year, but if plant management felt a project worthwhile, we bumped less meritorious ones to make room for them. We now make contingent allowances in the budget process for Quality Team projects.

EPILOGUE

All the Quality Team projects met the criteria set by the Local Steering Committee. More important, perhaps, they represent active participation by both hourly and supervisory employees in a process that is improving our product quality and competitive position. To date, this Quality Team effort reflects the success of the Committee.

A few lessons we have learned are:

- It would have been more effective to have the formal Quality Team structure in place when we first began training employees. We believe the refresher training we are currently providing will be more effective, because there is now a structure in which the training can be put to use.
- While it is important to have the commitment of top management, it is also a good idea to get all employees, including all supervisory levels, involved as soon as possible. We should have done this sooner.
- Training a larger number of willing people as statisticians, advisors, and "pushers" of the process would have been helpful from the outset.

Evolutionary Changes

Our Local Steering Committee has undergone several evolutionary changes. As more plant statisticians were trained, it became impractical for all of them to remain members of the Committee. We developed a rotation plan for membership that now includes six permanent seats for statisticians, with one position turning over each month.

Our statisticians, in fact, have been renamed Quality Improvement Advisors, in recognition of their growing expertise and role in the overall TQM process. They have formed a separate Quality Improvement Advisors Committee whose charter is to:

- Support the Local Steering Committee in the application of TQM philosophy.
- Coordinate the input of plant Advisors to the Local Steering Committee.
- Provide mutual support for and communications among the plant Advisors.
- Promote widespread use of statistical methodology.

This Committee meets at least monthly, and it has become an invaluable resource to us in guiding the plant program.

Our membership has also expanded to include five superintendent level positions in the maintenance, operating, and training functions, as a means of keeping middle management directly involved in the program.

There will undoubtedly be more changes, but the Local Steering Committee has been and remains the guiding force in our quality improvement program.

The Cost of Quality

Quality improvement has been, and will continue to be, an expensive program. While our accounting system does not track all costs specific to the program, our initial training, which represents the single largest out-of-pocket expense, exceeded a half-million dollars. These costs continue because normal attrition and the expansion of our plant and workforce have added new employees who need to be trained. Also, we are now holding refresher courses for all hourly employees, since their initial training was done four years ago.

If one were to judge the benefits of our program on a purely economic basis, it has been successful in that projects initiated by our Quality Teams have resulted in significant savings from improved equipment and process efficiencies, reduced generation of off-grade product, and less rework of product.

An example of this can be seen in one of our polyethylene products. To enhance its processability at our customer's plant, we inject it with a special additive with minimum–maximum specifications in the parts–per-million range. Using SPC, our operators quickly demonstrated that the process for injecting the additive was out of control. They were then able to convince supervision to rebuild the injection equipment with improvements suggested from their own experience. The results are twofold: much more uniform product quality going to the customer, and less off-grade production in our plant.

Improvements such as these represent production cost savings of about one million dollars *per year*, which will continue indefinitely. More significant is the fact that we have been improving the quality of the product going to our customers. But we now realize that opportunities for further improvement will always exist, and that quality improvement is in fact a never-ending process.

4

The TQM Coordinator

GERRY A. DAMON
Pearl Harbor Naval Shipyard

The TQM Coordinator coordinates the planning, implementation, and maintenance of the TQM effort. The Coordinator serves as the focal point for all the organization's TQM activities and monitors and manages the many processes associated with a planned change effort. Typically a middle manager, the Coordinator sits on the Executive Steering Committee and reports directly to the CEO or top manager (Figure 4.1). The Coordinator is *not* someone to whom the execution of quality has been solely delegated. That is management's responsibility. The Coordinator acts as the designated and highly visible change agent for TQM in the organization.

The TQM Coordinator's major responsibilities are to:

- Define and document TQM. Keep up-to-date on and maintain a working knowledge of the facts of TQM and organizational change.
- Act as the eyes and ears for the CEO or senior manager regarding the TQM effort, and help implement that effort.
- Regularly attend and participate in meetings of the Executive Steering Committee and Quality Leadership Teams.
- Arrange for and serve as secretary and facilitator for the Executive Steering Committee meetings.
- Prepare and coordinate the creation of a TQM implementation model and plan. Plan and schedule events and activities and monitor progress.

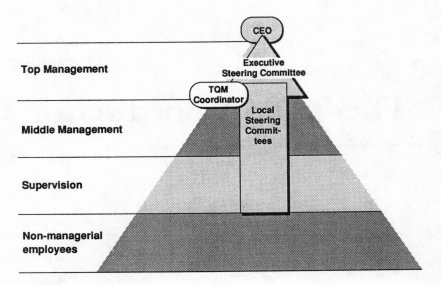

FIGURE 4.1

- Arrange for TQM training for all employees, and monitor its cost and effectiveness.
- Initiate, negotiate, and monitor contracts for consultants who assist in TQM implementation.
- Act as advisor and internal consultant to senior and line management on their role in supporting change.
- Assist, coordinate, and document the activities of Process Improvement (PI) Teams.
- Build organizational awareness about TQM and the change effort.

This chapter describes the office of the TQM Coordinator at Pearl Harbor Naval Shipyard.

PROFILE: PEARL HARBOR NAVAL SHIPYARD

Pearl Harbor Naval Shipyard (PHNSY), one of eight naval shipyards, currently has approximately 5,100 employees, including about forty top and middle managers (military personnel). The shipyard repairs and overhauls ships of the U.S. Navy, including surface and submarine, nuclear and non-nuclear. The production department makes up two-thirds of the shipyard and includes seventeen different trades and shops that comprise a variety of skilled workers, such as welders, shipfitters, pipe fitters, inside and outside machinists, sheet metal workers, electricians, and wood workers. The central union body for the shipyard is the Metal Trades Council, and our union membership numbers approximately 1,950.

TQM began in 1986 with the arrival of Captain Traister (now a two-star admiral) as our shipyard commander. Although a quality circle program was started in 1981, it had since dwindled to about five circles. Well read in Peter Drucker and Joe Juran, Captain Traister believed strongly in the idea of process improvement. With his initiation and the support of Larry Nelson, who was the QA director and a Deming advocate, the TQM effort began.

ESTABLISHING THE TQM OFFICE

In 1987, our next shipyard commander, Captain Coyle, visited Japan for two weeks to better understand what the Japanese were doing with Total Quality Control (TQC). Up to this point, his understanding of TQM had been limited to a Deming seminar, but the trip to Japan was a turning point for him. He saw that the Japanese management system included *Hoshin Kanri*, long-range planning that focuses a company's resources on a few high-priority issues. He also saw that the Japanese were very process-oriented: their work processes were defined, understood, and in control. The employees had hung on the walls charts of data and analyses of the projects on which they were working.

All this was in contrast to a shipyard that was struggling to repair and overhaul ships on time and within cost. The processes that supported our mission were not that well understood or in control. Measurements and indicators were not widely used to determine whether improvement was taking place or whether we were even going in the right direction.

Captain Coyle had observed that the Japanese typically have a separate office to promote TQM. Upon his return, he established a TQM Office in the shipyard, and I was assigned as the first full-time TQM Office Manager/Coordinator due to my previous experience with quality circles. This was followed by bringing in a secretary, a management analyst, a TQM trainer, and an industrial engineer. A year later, a statistician was brought on board and, after that, a second instructor to handle our increasing training workload.

RESPONSIBILITIES OF THE TQM COORDINATOR

The TQM Coordinator is responsible for communicating and clarifying what TQM is and how it is put into action. This is done by providing guidelines, directions, training, and working constantly to define and establish a TQM model, road map, and master plan that pull together the many elements of a quality improvement effort. Appointing a Coordinator guarantees that there will be someone with the time, experience, and background to serve as the focal point for an organization's TQM activities.

The responsibilities of the TQM Coordinator may vary for each organization and stage of the transformation. In our case, I conducted one-on-one interviews with our customers—namely, the shipyard's twenty-five department and office heads—in order to define their needs and the mission of the TQM Office. From this information, I determined the critical processes for which I would be responsible:

- Defining and planning the TQM implementation road map
- Developing and coordinating TQM training
- Promoting and publicizing the TQM effort
- Providing technical assistance in process improvement efforts
- Networking and serving as a central contact for TQM
- Supporting the Steering Committee and shipyard commander

To fulfill these various responsibilities, the TQM Coordinator needs training in statistical methods, the new management philosophy, facilitator skills, teambuilding, and any other courses or skills training available to managers. Conferences, such as GOAL/QPC in Boston, PACE in Philadelphia, and the ASQC, are also a valuable way to learn from the experiences of other organizations. Beyond the first two years, and depending on how TQM has evolved in the organization, additional training may include advanced statistics, Hoshin/Quality Planning, and the Seven New Management Tools.

Planning

Planning includes defining a road map and annual plan for implementing TQM, and a methodology for assessing our progress. The TQM Coordinator is responsible for defining, communicating, and gaining the Steering Committee's consensus on these elements.

Early on, our TQM implementation was ill-defined due to our lack of a road map. When we began TQM in 1986, there was much material available on philosophy and general principles written by the quality gurus, but there was not much literature of a practical, how-to nature about implementing TQM. We started developing a road map around general areas such as policy management, process management, and principle management (the Fourteen Points). The actual steps that these concepts entailed, however, were quite sketchy.

Today, we use ten key elements that GOAL/QPC outlines in their research reports as a framework for TQM implementation:

1. TQM Decision
2. Customer Focus
3. Critical Processes
4. Initial Teams
5. Five-Year Plan
6. Managing Momentum
7. Hoshin Planning
8. Daily Management
9. New Teams
10. Evaluating Progress

These ten elements serve as basic guidelines or mileposts to help us with TQM planning. Going to conferences and networking with our counterparts are also helpful ways to get ideas of what others are doing in terms of planning and coordinating TQM implementation. But problems with defining and implementing a road map from this framework are many. Budget cuts, downsizing, reorganization, and resistance problems are major factors that have required constant redefinition of how we implement TQM.

Evaluating our progress has been achieved through conducting an organizational climate survey and bringing in an advisor from Florida Power & Light to conduct a two-week assessment with managers and employees. This NAVSEA advisor, Captain Dan Pedrick, is a Naval Reserve officer who spends his reserve time meeting with the TQM principals from all the shipyards and performing these evaluations. His two-week assessment at PHNSY involved interviewing twenty-seven department and office heads about what they were doing with policy deployment, PI Teams, critical processes, and TQM process effectiveness (both today and long-range). From these interviews, he assembled an assessment of the shipyard's progress for the Steering Committee.

Training

The Coordinator is responsible for designing, developing, and coordinating TQM training. This involves working with outside consultants, developing the organization's own training and material, and scheduling instructors and training sessions. Initially, we used our external consultant to deliver training. This phase included training twenty-five PI Advisors/Internal Consultants, who would in turn train the shipyard managers.

There are three basic courses that we have developed:

1. "The New Management Philosophy" was originally delivered by the consultant. This three-day course provided the Steering Committee and the department and office heads with an introduction to TQM via Deming's Fourteen Points. We have since taken on the responsibility for this course, shortened it to two days, and assigned four managers to instruct it. This course is given primarily for new managers.
2. A three-day course in statistical tools is conducted by the two instructors in the TQM Office. This course is given quarterly for managers.
3. A two-day course in statistical methods is provided for the workforce. This particular course is coordinated and taught by our PI Advisors and supervisors, not by the TQM Office.

In addition to these basic internal courses, we now provide training for outside commands. Outside demand for training has expanded significantly over the last two years, and we now schedule an average of three to four courses or workshops each month for various government and Department of Defense commands, including Indonesia, Guam, Japan, Okinawa, and the Philippines. We have developed a three-day workshop on how to implement TQM, centering on customer focus, critical processes, and developing a strategic plan—in other words, how to translate general TQM concepts into concrete steps along the path.

We have also contracted many supplemental external training courses that have covered teambuilding, Hoshin planning, daily management, facilitator training, the Seven New Management Tools, and quality function deployment (QFD), a methodology for defining customer expectations and translating these requirements back to the work processes.

Promotion and Publicity

The Coordinator works to promote and publicize successes and progress both inside and outside the shipyard. The TQM Office provided some initial impetus to get publicity efforts going, but our public affairs office has bought into TQM and taken ownership of this function. They initiate a number of promotional activities, primarily the production of an in-house newspaper and videos.

The shipyard newspaper, "The Log," is the primary vehicle for recognizing team progress. This comes out every two weeks and almost always contains at least two TQM articles: a message from the shipyard commander on some aspect of TQM, and an update on one of the PI Teams, such as a success story about a particular department's process improvement project.

The videos that are produced every month link TQM with bottom-line waterfront indicators on the cost and schedule of ships currently in the shipyard. They show our progress on ships and the indicator charts that measure our progress. The videos also feature interviews with the workers on the deck plates, who tell how they see their work in relation to TQM. The videos are set up for viewing in a number of areas, such as the waterfront, the training building, and in each department.

In addition to the public affairs office, most departments have their own newsletters and display areas for performance indicators. Storyboard displays of team projects and other activities are posted at a display area of the training building.

Technical Assistance

The TQM Office responds to various requests from departments to help them in some aspect of process improvement. Typically, these questions come to our statistician from PI Advisors when they need greater statistical expertise for the projects and teams with which they're working. Departments need help on how to conduct surveys, what data to collect, and how to analyze and evaluate the data. This also involves developing measurements and indicators that reflect how well the department is achieving its mission and meeting customer needs. The supply department, for example, is continuously working to develop indicators that show how well they're getting the right material to the right place at the right time.

Networking

The Coordinator is the central contact for TQM both inside and outside the organization. Networking with my counterparts has provided a valuable forum for sharing approaches, ideas, and the lessons we've learned. This takes place at two levels. At the national level, the TQM principals for the eight naval shipyards meet quarterly to work on implementing TQM consistently at all the shipyards and at headquarters in Washington, D.C. At the local level in Hawaii, Government Organizations Together for Quality (GOT-Q) was formed to share information and resources. Both the national and local groups have similar visions of developing and providing TQM leadership for their commands. They are actually a form of user group in which we practice using the tools of TQM. For example, by working on a strategic plan for the group, we can teach and develop the skills needed for leadership roles at our own commands. "Walking our talk" must always be one of our guiding principles.

Supporting the Executive Steering Committee

The TQM Coordinator attends Executive Steering Committee meetings, provides agendas, and records and distributes the minutes. This support role also involves responding to action items and scheduling top management progress reviews with the shipyard commander.

The specific duties involved here are quite diverse, such as working on TQM presentations and coordinating communications from the shipyard commander and the Steering Committee to the individual departments. A current example of this is drafting the Steering Committee's action plan for the department and office heads to develop their own mission and vision statements.

The executive assistant for the shipyard commander puts together operations plan progress reviews for the shipyard, which is an important function that feeds into our planning process. These progress reviews are a measure of how well we are meeting the overall strategic plan issued from Washington headquarters. This requires meeting with the functional area managers to see how they're doing in various areas, such as process improvement and strategic planning, and reviewing these reports at the Steering Committee meetings.

LEARNING ALONG THE WAY

As we provide training and workshops for both our own shipyard and external commands, questions always arise about what problems we have encountered, what mistakes we have made that others should look out for. There are a number of lessons we have learned:

- *Awareness training should be provided to everyone.* Be cautioned, however, that when you train all employees, you raise their expectations. Be prepared to follow through and deliver.
- *Training in SPC is most useful and cost-efficient when provided on a just-in-time basis.* We relied heavily on mass training at first, but the best time for training is when teams or groups are formed and have defined a problem or project to study and improve. This lets them immediately apply the tools they have learned to real problems.
- *Develop a road map for TQM implementation early on.* If the Executive Steering Committee does not have a plan or framework for TQM, the effort becomes one of confusion and wasted time.
- *The task side of TQM is much easier than the people side.* Old behaviors die hard, and managers will continue to point fingers and blame the other guy. It is the unusual manager who practices what is preached. Expecting all managers and supervisors to be transformed through the training experience is unrealis-

tic. The culture change takes time, and people need time to practice TQM concepts before TQM becomes a way of conducting everyday business.

• *Dig where the ground is soft*. Identify and work with the twenty percent who are receptive to TQM, rather than the sixty percent who are on the fence or the other twenty percent who are not receptive. We have found that the ones who are receptive will make it work and convince some of the sixty percent to join in. Don't waste your time with the twenty percent who resist. Triage must be a way of life if you are to survive.

Working with the Union

Another lesson we continue to learn is the importance of labor-management cooperation. In 1987, when we hired a consultant to help us in the implementation process, we were strongly encouraged to accept the union as equal partners in TQM. Consequently, management invited the union to participate and, for several years, they were represented on the Executive Steering Committee plus the forty-some other Local Steering Committees in the various departments, offices, and shops.

This new labor-management relationship was not without difficulty. The union participants on these committees found it difficult not to be perceived by their members as "in bed with management." To help in this regard, we established a separate labor-management committee to address union concerns about TQM. Although there were rough spots as these two groups came together, most felt that relations improved markedly. It was during this time that the union provided a number of excellent ideas for improving TQM implementation, and labor-management cooperation was generally considered a success.

One of the union's ideas came at a time when the TQM effort was starting to lose steam and level off, and we needed new impetus to keep going. One union official recommended that an executive-level person (higher than the TQM Coordinator) be appointed to promote TQM in the shipyard. This resulted in naming an executive assistant to the shipyard commander, which showed top management's renewed and strengthened commitment to the TQM effort.

This labor-management relationship continued until a new union president was elected in 1990, and the union withdrew from further participation. Several factors contributed to this withdrawal. The new president and some stewards were not happy about the degree of progress and felt that TQM was not working. Second, the national union was strongly discouraging local participation and had issued a "white paper" negating all support of TQM. This has resulted in a strained labor-management relationship at present, but it illustrates the need to understand the difficult political role that union leaders must play. The appearance of being co-opted by management is a real danger.

EPILOGUE

All in all, we have made some significant gains at PHNSY. We have had over five hundred PI Teams that have generated some notable improvements and cost savings in the range of millions of dollars. It can be difficult, however, to translate this to bottom-line results. For one thing, TQM implementation is not complete. Second, there are many other factors at play. The effects of budget cuts, downsizing, and the reorganization of all the shipyards make it difficult to isolate and measure the success of TQM.

Our mission is to repair and overhaul ships of the U.S. Navy on time and within cost. Quality is a given. Our strategy is to put into place a two-part quality management system. The first part includes our shipyard operations plan, which is made up of our mission, vision, goals, and objectives. To achieve our mission and vision through the goals and objectives, we must deploy this plan to all levels of shipyard management down to the first-line level. When we get all levels doing their part to contribute to this overall plan, we will improve our overall shipyard performance and be successful.

The second part of our quality management system involves the establishment of a daily management control system. Again, managers at each management level must identify their customers and their needs. The next step is to identify the critical processes that produce the products and services that meet these needs. Finally, only by continuously improving these processes and monitoring the performance indicators will we be successful in delighting our customers, which is the only purpose of any job.

5

The Quality Leadership Team

JOHN B. ROGERS
Zytec Corporation

Quality Leadership Teams are formed to improve the quality of management processes. The teams represent a diagonal slice through the organization, each one consisting of six to twelve managers and employees from various functional areas and levels (Figure 5.1). Elected union leadership should also be included where appropriate. All members are peers in the sense that no one should report to anyone else on the team. The composition of the team should provide a broad spectrum of ideas about how to create an environment that more fully empowers employees so they can better contribute to the organization's mission and values. The organization may charter as many teams as necessary to improve management processes.

The Quality Leadership Team's major responsibilities are to:

- Identify barriers and roadblocks in policies and procedures that limit the full participation of employees.
- Work with the Executive and Local Steering Committees to establish efforts and plans for removing these barriers.
- Monitor all efforts to ensure that barriers are permanently removed.
- Be an ongoing vehicle for promoting the organization's values and principles.

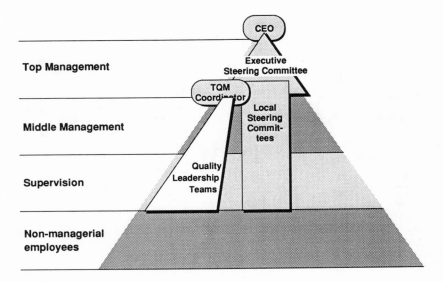

FIGURE 5.1

This chapter describes the efforts of the Zytec Corporation, which uses the term Deming Implementation Team (DIT) for their Quality Leadership Teams.

PROFILE: ZYTEC CORPORATION

Zytec Corporation was founded in 1984 to take over the power supply operation of Magnetic Peripherals, Inc., a subsidiary of Control Data Corporation. Zytec manufactures custom-designed switching power supplies for customers who make computers, office equipment, medical electronic devices, test equipment, and telecommunication switches. Zytec employs nearly six hundred people, and has operations in Eden Prairie and Redwood Falls, Minnesota.

In 1984, the management of Zytec decided to adopt the principles of Dr. Deming in an effort to raise quality to a level that would make the company competitive in world markets. The TQM movement was in its infancy when the company was formed, but quality was the strategic thrust of Zytec's original business plan. The reasoning was that a U.S. company can't compete on the basis of low price, but it can compete on know-how. At this time, Deming's ideas were brought to Zytec's strategic planning meeting by John Steel, the vice president of marketing and sales. The strategic planning group, then consisting of senior management and about twenty key engineers and managers from throughout the company, agreed that Deming's principles provided a good foundation upon which to build a quality organization striving for continuous improvement. As a result of this planning session, our CEO, Ron Schmidt, adopted the program with a single-mindedness that precluded its being dropped, diluted, or substantially modified.

Zytec's first action was to send eleven employees to a Deming seminar. The CEO established an Executive Steering Committee consisting of those who reported directly to him. This group established a champion for each of Deming's Fourteen Points. After the seminar, the strategic planning group rated Zytec's implementation of the Fourteen Points as fairly poor: on a scale of 1 to 10, our highest mark was 4 in constancy of purpose.

It was clear from the start that Deming's philosophy would not be easy to communicate to all employees. The philosophy is so different from time-honored American practices that it must be fairly comprehensively understood to make sense. Indeed, some of our initial actions were straightforward responses to the Fourteen Points but did not make a lot of sense on the factory floor. For example, our first major step was to discontinue inspection (point 3) and develop an SPC course for all employees (point 6). We reassigned the inspectors to other positions and began the process of self-inspection. At first, this caused employees to wonder whether we could produce a quality product without inspectors. In light of experience, the tactic was crazy; in light of Deming principles, it was sound and fundamental.

It became obvious that all employees first had to understand the philosophy of TQM for us to make the transformation successfully. At this time, we sent seventy-nine employees to a seminar given by our external consultant. This was a major commitment for our company to make during a time of financial hardship.

DEMING IMPLEMENTATION TEAMS

The Executive Steering Committee recognized that the transformation must be accomplished at all levels of the organization, and that it alone did not have the time or expertise to carry out implementation. The Committee decided to establish Quality Leadership Teams, which we called Deming Implementation Teams (DITs), for a concentrated study of the Fourteen Points. Because of the many interrelationships among the points, three DITs were formed. Each team would study one of three common themes: philosophy, policy, and practices.

1. The Fundamentals DIT covered points 1, 2, 5, and 14. This group would focus on fundamental company philosophy.
2. The Policy DIT covered points 3, 4, 6, 7, and 13.
3. The Practices DIT covered points 8, 9, 10, 11, and 12.

The Steering Committee defined the tasks of these teams to be analytical, but it also expected them to suggest ways of carrying their points into action.

The structure of the DITs reflected the Steering Committee's recognition that it is essential to have senior management continuously involved in the implementation process. The Steering Committee consisted of the company's seven senior staff members. Although the director of quality was both a member of that staff and the coordinator for ongoing TQM efforts, it was felt that all of the senior staff needed to stay in on the process. The DITs, on the other hand, were selected from all levels of the company. One Steering Committee member was assigned to be the champion for each DIT. This champion would serve as the liaison to the senior staff and find resources to accomplish the plans of the DIT.

Team Members

The Steering Committee recognized that each DIT needed a certain critical mass of information about the company and the company's policies. The Committee selected the original DIT members from the group that had been to seminars given by Deming or our external consultant. Our intent was to balance knowledge, management levels, disciplines, and personalities, while recognizing the differences in orientation of these issues:

- The Fundamentals DIT got mostly managers, because these points tend to be general and philosophical.
- The Policies DIT was split evenly between management and

line workers, because these points address company policies and need the consensus of all categories of workers.
- The Practices DIT was made up primarily of non-managers, because these points tend to be pragmatic and action-oriented.

Subsequent natural change in membership largely erased these differences in composition. One of the liaison Steering Committee members observed that the groups would be better formed if based on the personalities of the people instead of their organizational position. In any case, the original composition of the groups did not seem to impede progress. The choice of DIT members seems to have been a good one: it gave the Steering Committee the option to insure knowledge, energy, and activism, and to mix people who would not normally work with each other. Our tendency to stratify by management classification was perhaps spurious, but not negative.

There was quite a bit of initial enthusiasm, particularly from the manufacturing organization, and all employees were encouraged to volunteer for the groups. Initially, we had more volunteers than we thought we could use, given our desire to keep the groups to a reasonable size (under fifteen).

Training Program

Since few had been given training initially, we had to explain the TQM process not only to incoming group members but also to the company. The Steering Committee developed a training program using Deming's book *Quality, Productivity, and Competitive Position*. This was first given to all managers, primarily to refamiliarize them. The managers and volunteer Committee members then trained each manager's work group so that, over a period of several months, all employees had an overview of TQM principles and a statement of Zytec's intention to use the DIT groups to instill those principles throughout the company.

Leaders and Liaisons

The Steering Committee did not specify agendas for each of the DITs, although some suggestions were made. One member of the Committee was also assigned to each DIT as a liaison who would be an official observer, reporting to the Committee and requesting needed resources. In practice, the liaison often became an active member of the DIT and its champion on the Committee.

The Committee had specified that DIT leaders would be elected by the members and that leadership would change every six months. The liaisons did not become leaders, but they did participate in the groups to a greater extent than had been foreseen. In general, having an elected leader and an appointed liaison seems to have worked well, allowing the DITs considerable autonomy, guaranteeing good communication, and ensuring that no one worked at cross-purposes to the Committee.

Group Meetings

The DITs were enthusiastic, each taking on different characteristics based on their assigned points and their own personalities. They initially met as often as weekly, usually for two to four hours. As the groups matured, meetings became less frequent. Our meetings may be longer than optimum because of our geographical limitations: all groups have members from two company locations about two hours apart. While meetings can sometimes be conducted by teleconference, most meetings are face-to-face. Given the travel time, we tended to schedule meetings less frequently with more homework assignments to individual group members.

EARLY IDEAS

Some of the DITs' early efforts were very successful, others not so much. Some of these ideas were to:

- *Develop a Values Statement to explain how and why we do business.* This was written by the Fundamentals DIT and published as a booklet. We still use this Values Statement, and it has proved very successful in explaining ourselves both internally and externally. For example, the statement is given to all new employees, and it establishes the structure of the first part of their training. An abridged form of the statement is posted widely throughout the company. This constant repetition of our values is not the kind of exhortation that Deming cautions against, however; it is a statement of principles, not a directive or an instruction.

- *Use an Ishikawa diagram to break down communication barriers between departments.* This was an ambitious project for the Practices DIT. The group posted a CEDAC diagram (cause-and-effect diagram with the addition of cards) in the company's lunchrooms and let employees add ideas. This was a bare fishbone diagram together with a pad of Post-it™ Notes, on which employees could write comments and stick them on the appropriate line of the diagram. The exercise provided some new ways to break down barriers. Perhaps as important, it reminded employees of the existence of these groups and publicized the use of CEDAC as a problem-solving technique.
- *Pay the direct labor force based on knowledge, rather than current job definition or service.* This was a profound change suggested by the Policy DIT. The idea was to break up the work of manufacturing a power supply into a series of specific tasks: use of the wave solder machine, final assembly of the power supply, and so on. Each task would entail corresponding training, such as component identification or soldering. After spending a required amount of time in the task, an employee would take a hands-on test to demonstrate the ability to create high-quality work at this task. The immediate and obvious concern of the worker group was the testing: Would it be fair? What would be tested? Was the time requirement fair? Still, the idea seems to have been more readily accepted because it came from a DIT group.
- *Adopt profit sharing.* The Fundamentals DIT put in quite a bit of time designing a specific plan. At the time, the company was not in the financial position to offer profit sharing, so the effort—at least the detailed design effort—was wasted. The group was disappointed to have put in great effort only to be refused. However, the group did make its presentation to the Steering Committee, and the reason for refusal was clear and agreed upon. There has been no residual ill will between the group and the Steering Committee, and the issue of profit sharing is still very much alive.

In addition to the DITs, we decided to use employee teams for other evaluation and policy projects. The primary area in which this was done early on was establishing a task group to investigate the pay-for-knowledge idea. This became known as the Multi Functional

Employee (MFE) task group. The group invested a great deal of time in determining the process by which an employee would accomplish new tasks, get certified, and be paid. The group explained the process to Zytec's first-line managers and initiated the MFE concept company-wide in 1987.

A number of serious problems developed almost immediately. The line managers, not having been trained in-depth in the process, administered it differently, causing employees to feel unfairly treated. Second, as the situation got worse, managers stopped giving employees the required examinations for task accomplishment. Many employees felt that the promise of MFE would never be realized.

Finally, a second MFE task group was formed. This group, comprised primarily of line employees, was well promoted. Most or all employees who signed up were accepted into the group, which had thirty-seven participants at its highest point. This task group labored for months and produced successful modifications to the original system. However, it was only after most people dropped out of the group—many of them frustrated because a leaderless group of so many people has a hard time accomplishing anything—that about ten diehards fell together and began making the necessary changes.

The testing portion of task attainment was now to be administered by a group of employees with the manager's input. This allowed the manager to handle more tests on a more consistent basis. The testing procedure itself was "normalized" across all tasks, so that employees' knowledge of quality systems and desire to learn became tested attributes, as was their hands-on ability to do the job. The current MFE system operates well (the only criticism is that it grants task certification too early), and the MFE group continues to meet.

Lessons from the First Phase

We learned a number of lessons from the first phase of DITs:

- There is a vast reservoir of creativity and good ideas in the company. The best of the team results were truly impressive. The Values Statement is clear and well written, and has survived three years without change. The MFE concept was a true innovation. The use of the fishbone diagram helped make analytical techniques an everyday thing at Zytec.
- People need to know what's needed. For example, profit shar-

ing was a good idea, but the group did not understand that Zytec was not then in a financial position to execute it.

- The "open system" approach, in which all volunteers are encouraged to get involved, is a good way of inculcating knowledge about TQM principles throughout the company. It's not, however, such a good way to run a meeting.
- Members of the original groups all mentioned that they needed skills they hadn't had before. While the first groups were operating, our training department developed several courses: Making Meetings Work, Problem Solving, Listening Skills, Dealing with Conflict, as well as the Seven Basic Tools taught in the SPC course. Over half of our employees have taken one or more of these courses.

AFTER THE FIRST YEAR

After about a year, the DITs had addressed the initial objectives and obvious tasks. The Steering Committee felt that the teams had served the company well. Membership on the teams, which had originally been controlled by the Steering Committee, had rolled over, so that over one hundred people had been involved in the team process in one way or another. Those people formed the nucleus of a communication infrastructure for making TQM concepts make sense to the company.

The Steering Committee's original idea was to cut the teams loose, let them define their own work, and ultimately build all Fourteen Points into the company. As the teams changed membership and ran through their own original agendas, interest in the meetings began to flag. It seemed that the groups began to strain for good ideas and, in a couple cases, began parallel efforts on the same problem. There seem to have been two reasons for this:

1. The Steering Committee had to maintain a delicate balance between a directive approach, which would have guaranteed an efficient process, and operating in a hands-off fashion to encourage maximum participation. The Committee operated in a hands-off fashion at first, and the groups enthusiastically burned through many creative and interesting ideas. As the groups matured, ideas that could be acted on were harder to come by.

2. The logistics of the process were more difficult than they originally appeared. As mentioned above, members of the original groups needed skills in communications, listening, and
   meeting-mechanics to which many had not been exposed.

The Steering Committee recognized these problems and responded on two fronts: it moved from a hands-off to a more directive approach, assigning the teams to high-priority projects; and it
arranged for specific training to be available to all employees. In retrospect, the Steering Committee would not have acted differently in
its overall approach. The initial hands-off attitude strongly encouraged employee participation, and it made clear the company's intention to put everybody to work on the transformation.

In addition to inculcating TQM principles in the company, the
group members provided a pool of knowledgeable people for specific tasks the company needed to solve. It was about this time that
the company formed a task group to look at evaluation and pay for
nondirect labor. Zytec had used a management-by-objective (MBO)
system and saw the need to get rid of it. The task group was formed
by the personnel director, though it was not dominated by the personnel department. The group met often during late 1986 and 1987,
and invested a great deal of time on an innovative product called
the Analysis of Job Responsibilities.

Designed around the PDCA Cycle, the Analysis of Job Responsibilities designated individual job responsibilities (in essence, a job
description), the customers for each element of responsibility, the
desired outcomes of accomplishing each responsibility at high quality, and an open area for ongoing status reporting. The purpose of
this system was to move from the arbitrary, long-term nature of most
traditional coaching systems to an employee-driven, short-cycle system that encourages continuous improvement.

The group also proposed that pay be separated from evaluation,
and that pay increases be simplified to a single dollar figure for each
pay range for all but exceptional and poor performers. The process
was written by the group and introduced to all nondirect workers in
1986.

Setting Priorities

After several months of slowing activity in the groups, the Steering
Committee met to evaluate how to improve them. The Committee

brainstormed all the tasks necessary for becoming a TQM company. We then eliminated those ideas that were in process somewhere in the company, and used weighted voting to set priorities on the remaining points. The high priorities were then given to the three teams as suggestions for further activity.

- The Practices DIT was assigned SPC implementation and was asked to develop a training curriculum for the company.
- The Policy DIT was given the task of designing a skills training curriculum for each employee.
- The Fundamentals DIT was assigned the job of reevaluating and updating the Analysis of Job Responsibilities, which had been in operation for over a year at this time. Although the system was universally admired, it was not being widely used. (Subsequent surveys concluded that it was not being used because it was voluntary.)

These assignments resulted in a renaissance of activity on the teams.

As this second round of team tasks ended, the Steering Committee felt that the approach of driving TQM through the company point-by-point had been successful. Enough awareness now existed so that the company could change its focus from the points per se to the specific skills and processes for improving quality.

The teams are currently inactive while the Steering Committee determines the next step in the process. A random sample of the entire company taken in early 1990 showed substantial progress toward our goal, though there is clearly room for more (Figure 5.2).

LEARNING ALONG THE WAY

Zytec learned a number of things along the way.

With all its errors and inefficiencies, the process of involving the whole company—with no detailed plan of action, no controlling agenda, no grading of what was best—was a good idea. The teams bred some pros who now understand TQM in a real, pragmatic way. They can explain the principles and demonstrate them in action, making the ideas real for other employees.

Each company's implementation of the principles is different.

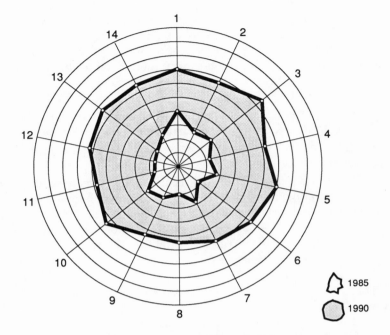

FIGURE 5.2   Zytec's progress toward the Fourteen Points.

The principles themselves are abstract and become real only when they are interpreted in the context of a company's operating reality. The teams helped build a set of TQM operating principles at Zytec.

The hard part of implementing TQM is not the decision to do so, but the execution of it. It is absolutely essential that top management be firmly and clearly committed to supporting the time, the energy, and the changes necessary to becoming a TQM company. The job is so difficult, and we realize that we have just begun a journey that will never end.

We learned that team members have good and creative ideas, but that they need training to be effective. Also, all the rules of good meetings still pertain: groups should be smaller than they often are, meetings should have agendas or they wander, and so on.

We learned that if we ask employees to operate independently and creatively, they need a larger tool kit of techniques and a substantially broader understanding of the company's objectives. The

Steering Committee recognized this and began developing a training program for all employees in 1987. This training, called Zytec Involved People (ZIP) is a sixteen-hour interactive statement of Zytec's values and operating principles. We invested over nine thousand hours in this, because we knew that TQM is so different from traditional American business practices that the overall program is hard for most people to understand. Also, although it was not a direct outcome of the DITs, the company adopted a method of long-range planning called Management By Planning (MBP), based on the Japanese process Hoshin Kanri, which emphasizes a sharing of strategic objectives and a response to those objectives by teams involving all employees. MBP was built by senior management, but it was the active role of the DITs that provided a model for interactive management and process development, and made MBP easy from an organizational/cultural point of view.

Finally, we recognize that once the investment in time and training is made, the company must be open to accepting the changes suggested by the groups. This can be difficult. Employees who do not fully understand the company's objectives or TQM principles, or who carry personal crusades through group meetings, can come up with unacceptable options. In practice, this did not turn out to be a major problem at Zytec. The Steering Committee rejected profit sharing out of financial necessity, but was careful to explain its reasons so that the group understood and accepted the decision. Despite this rejection, there was a valuable forum on the topic, and profit sharing remains part of our strategic plan.

By investing employee groups with the right to generate solutions, a corporation creates a dilemma for itself if it does not adequately prepare the employees for the job. If the Steering Committee rejects ideas for reasons deemed insufficient by the groups, we seriously undermine the implementation of TQM. On the other hand, if the Steering Committee accepts ideas that are ineffective or contrary to company strategies, the company suboptimizes its own resources. We know of only one solution: prepare the people. Perhaps we did not understand the depth of that commitment when we began. It must be a major strategic focus to be successful.

If Zytec had to start the process all over again, we would probably do some things differently, but not many. The group members generally felt positive that the company was finally asking them to use their minds to improve the company. Many became frustrated from time to time with inefficient meetings, domineering team members, and groups that were too large. All participants, however, felt the teams had been positive on the balance.

The Steering Committee discussed whether it should manage the DITs more closely, particularly after the first rush of enthusiasm. It was concluded that they would not. The teams need leadership, not management. When the process is not led, it can become wasteful. The teams and middle management were perhaps more concerned than the Steering Committee about the efficiency of the groups. However, closer management might well have prevented several of the really creative ideas from coming out, particularly if it had been "more of the same" management.

OUR ADVICE

Our experience—our successes, failures, and adjustments—can be read accurately only in the context of our culture. What we think we can say to a company contemplating TQM is:

- Top management—the CEO—must be fully committed before the program starts. The process is difficult, time-consuming, and expensive. It takes several years, and if the CEO's commitment wavers, the program risks becoming just another one of those management programs.
- Train upper management in the TQM philosophy. Management must support the philosophy consistently if it is to spread throughout the company.
- Train, train, train. People must operate from a base of knowledge. They must know how to solve problems, how to run meetings, what the company wants, and what resources can be devoted to their ideas.
- Bring in a process consultant—someone not tied to the company and its specific problems—to keep your focus on getting the job done.
- Start early. Teams should begin as soon as the company is committed and understands the investment. In their initial phases, they will spend quite a bit of time getting the training required to carry out their jobs. It would be understandable if teams take more than a year to produce results, but some re-

sults are needed sooner than that. Thus, start the training early, even if not everybody knows about TQM and SPC.

- Let the Quality Leadership Teams drive themselves at first. It will be apparent when they get into trouble. When they do get into trouble, focus the mission. A narrow focus is conducive to clearer results. For example, our experience indicates that setting up one team to address all of the Fourteen Points would not work.
- Be careful about team mechanics. Select members who will provide a strong knowledge base on the subject matter (for example, include a personnel specialist in a discussion about compensation), keep the groups to a practical size (fewer than ten attendees at most meetings), train leaders in effective operation of meetings, and so on. For many people, this will be the first cooperative, consensus-building effort in which they have been involved. Sticking to the basics is essential.

On the balance, involving the people in creating the Quality Leadership Teams was a good method of carrying TQM concepts throughout the company. It required great strength and purpose on the part of the CEO and the Steering Committee, since the large time commitment had to be borne during a time when the company was suffering financial growing pains. But the Steering Committee and the group members can't think of a way that we could otherwise have accomplished the grass-roots knowledge, understanding, and acceptance. The positive result is that we have harnessed our employees' creative energy, and the process has permanently added to the value of our employees. The first leg of our journey was difficult, but has paid for itself already.

Postscript

In September 1991, Zytec became the first recipient of the Minnesota Quality Award. In October 1991, Zytec was one of only three winners of the Malcolm Baldrige National Quality Award for that year.

6

The Process Improvement Advisor

MICHAEL S. THOMAS
Chevron Pipe Line Company

Process Improvement (PI) Advisors are selected from the organization's current hourly or salaried employees—or even managers—for their ability to learn and teach the tools of SPC and process improvement (Figure 6.1). These people should have the desire to become fully trained in process improvement methods, the willingness to teach and coach others in their application, and the ability to gain acceptance and credibility with peers and superiors. The organization should select and train enough PI Advisors to meet their training and coaching needs.

The Advisor's major responsibilities are to:

- Learn, apply, and teach process improvement methods, including problem-solving techniques and SPC.
- Initiate, facilitate, and coordinate PI Team activities at a local level.
- Act as a coach and mentor to people in the organization who need help or advice with process improvement efforts.
- Work with Local Steering Committees to identify process improvement opportunities.

This chapter describes the function of PI Advisors at Chevron Pipe Line Company.

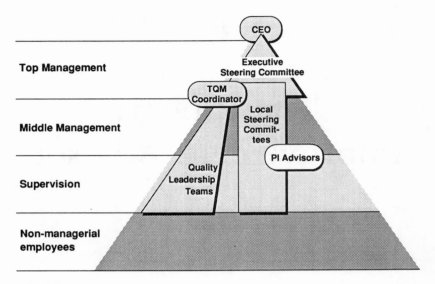

FIGURE 6.1

PROFILE: CHEVRON PIPE LINE COMPANY

Chevron Pipe Line Company (CPL), a subsidiary of Chevron Corporation, is a common-carrier transporter of raw petroleum liquids, refined products, chemicals, and gas. Over half of our business is with other Chevron operating companies, such as Chevron U.S.A. (CUSA), Warren Petroleum, and Chevron Chemical. Chevron Chemical initiated a TQM effort in the mid-1980s, driven by the needs of one of their major customers. Awareness and interest in quality grew throughout the Chevron family of companies, and CPL started its TQM effort in 1988.

Because CPL interacts with virtually every phase of the business, we are in a unique position to spread the awareness of the need to improve quality. In transporting crude oil and liquified petroleum gas, CUSA and Warren Petroleum are our suppliers and the refineries are our customers. In transporting refined products, the refineries are our suppliers and the marketing department is our customer. The need for constancy of purpose is crucial among the many players in this extended process.

THE ROLE OF PROCESS IMPROVEMENT (PI) ADVISORS

The TQM transformation requires fundamental changes in the way people work at all levels of the organization. This change begins with the awareness, commitment, and actions of top management, which must provide the resources to train both themselves and all employees. As the transformation proceeds, employees at every level must become involved. PI Advisors are key to this process as they develop and deploy a profound knowledge of process improvement methods.

During the initial phase of the transformation, there are several reasons to train PI Advisors:

- The initial training and consulting efforts are extensive and require the involvement of many people, but it may not be practical to bring aboard a large number of external consultants.
- Advisors come into the game with the home field advantage. They already understand the culture, know the business, and have good working relationships throughout the organization. These relationships, built on trust, are important elements in beginning the change process.
- Advisors can provide training and internal consulting to help spread the knowledge needed throughout the organization during the first few years of the transformation. When the organization has made TQM a way of life, both external and internal consultants such as PI Advisors may no longer be needed.

Three Roles of the PI Advisor

PI Advisors play three important roles:

1. As an Applications Consultant, an Advisor helps teams use process improvement methods in their work.
2. As a Process Improvement Methods (PIM) Instructor, an Advisor teaches process improvement methods to employees, both in the classroom and within teams.
3. As an Internal Consultant, an Advisor helps Steering Com-

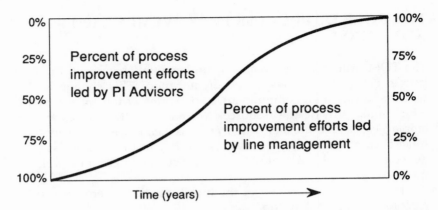

FIGURE 6.2   The transition from PI Advisor to line management.

mittees, teams, and individuals identify and resolve tough issues in implementing TQM.

PI Advisors have various capabilities and experiences that may
suit them for particular roles. All Advisors start as Applications Consultants. Some may continue to do only applications consulting, while
others with teaching skills will go on to become PIM Instructors.
Some will develop a knack for identifying and addressing tough issues, such as barriers to progress in the corporate culture. These are
the people who can become Internal Consultants.

These primary roles are similar among all organizations. What
does vary greatly, however, are the methods they use, which depend on the organization's particular customers, values, culture,
business objectives, processes, and opportunities.

Most of our PI Advisors remained in their existing positions,
which provided them a testing ground for applying process improvement methods in their familiar job functions. This created quite
a work overload, and management support was needed to shift some
of their existing workload. As PI Advisors, they typically "report"
to the leader of the Steering Committee with which they work. In
their normal functions, they typically continue reporting to their
functional supervisors.

The role of the PI Advisor is not intended to be a position. The
initial stages of the TQM transformation involve rapid deployment
of a large body of knowledge over a relatively short period of time.

People must be educated in the new way of doing business, and they need help applying this knowledge to their work. Initially, the Advisors carry the lion's share of training and coaching teams in their process improvement efforts. These roles are gradually adopted by line management, as supervisors and managers learn to lead the teams. Figure 6.2 shows this transition to line management.

SELECTING AND DEVELOPING PI ADVISORS

The process we use to select and develop Advisors follows the PDCA Cycle, as shown in Figure 6.3 and explained in the sections that follow.

Defining the Purpose and Roles

When CPL began the TQM transformation, we were not entirely clear just what the PI Advisors would actually do. We knew that the transformation would take us years, but, being action-oriented managers, we wanted to get the whole thing rolling all at once. As a result, we selected and trained PI Advisors before we had figured out their role in the transformation. Many of the problems we encountered stemmed from this all all-at-once approach.

At first, we expected all Advisors to handle whatever training and team consulting were required. It was early 1990 before we defined the three roles of the Advisor and realized that different levels of training were required. There was also substantial confusion between the role of a supervisor/team leader and that of the PI Advisor. This stemmed partly from not having defined the role of supervisors in a transformed organization.

Our experience underscores the need for top management to take the time to clearly define the purpose of the transformation and the roles of all the players. To be effective, PI Advisors must know how they fit into the overall plan. The Executive Steering Committee must define the criteria for Advisors, which the Local Steering Committees can then use for selecting the right candidates.

The Executive Steering Committee must also decide how many Advisors are needed. It may be best to start out small: training too many up front can cause frustration and chaos, while training too few can overload the ones who are trained. A starting point might be:

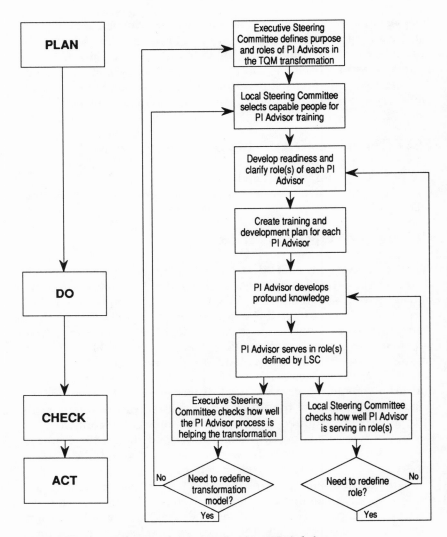

FIGURE 6.3   Selecting and developing PI Advisors.

- One Internal Consultant for each Steering Committee.
- At least two PIM Instructors for each geographical business unit or division. Team teaching works well for us, and we recommend pairing up.

- An Applications Consultant for each functional or geographical area.

CPL selected and trained twelve PI Advisors to start with: two in each of our five divisions (with 100 to 200 employees per division), and two in the home office. We assumed that the Advisors could attend three weeks of training, provide instruction and team consulting, and still find time to perform their regular job functions. Our best guess was that this extra work would take twenty to fifty percent of their time.

Part of the rationale to keep PI Advisors in their existing jobs was to let them apply their newly acquired skills to familiar work processes. Another reason for keeping them in their current jobs was our uncertainty about what to do with them when their PI Advisor roles were finished.

Before long, the Advisors who took their roles seriously (by far the majority) found themselves rapidly overloaded. Some managers provided temporary replacements and put the PI Advisors on quality full-time. Other managers trained more "part-time" PI Advisors. Both of these approaches reduced the overload somewhat, and we trained seventeen more PI Advisors during the second year of the transformation.

Selecting Capable PI Advisors

The Local Steering Committee should select employees who have a natural talent for the role of PI Advisor. This selection should not be taken lightly. Several years into the TQM transformation, it becomes evident that the skills and leadership qualities of the Applications Consultant are needed by all supervisors. Likewise, the profound knowledge and skills of the Internal Consultant are needed by managers to lead and support their people. The initial selection of Advisors should take into account how these roles will eventually be integrated within the organization. Selecting supervisors and managers can be valuable, because their involvement can simplify the change process in middle management.

Our experience shows several characteristics to be good indicators of successful PI Advisors. In general, they:

- Are trusted and respected by co-workers and management, and naturally sought out for advice. They have granted, rather than vested, authority.

- Communicate effectively with people of varied background and experience.
- Have some mathematical and problem-solving abilities—enough to learn and teach simple statistical methods.
- Can commit at least twenty-five to fifty percent of their time to the quality effort for at least a year. After that, the time commitment may increase or decrease.
- Are interested and excited about the opportunity.
- Are creative, like to experiment, and are willing to take informed risks.

Three of our first PI Advisors were line supervisors. These may have been the best selections, because they were in positions where they could most directly apply the quality principles they were learning. Four of the Advisors were division training coordinators, who greatly helped in the rapid deployment of training for all company employees in the first year and a half of the transformation. (Unfortunately, training was deployed a bit too rapidly.) The other five Advisors were in non-supervisory technical positions. These people were successful largely because they were selected for their natural talents, not their position.

By the third year, we began to realize it was the managers and supervisors who should become PI Advisors. Approximately eighty managers and supervisors attended the basic PI Advisor training, beginning with the Executive Steering Committee, then the Local Steering Committee, and then extending to all supervisors. This reflects our current approach to rolling out training from the top down.

Developing Readiness and Clarifying Roles

Management must support PI Advisors before, during, and after their training. The Local Steering Committee ensures that PI Advisors understand:

- Their role before they begin training.
- What training they will receive and how they will apply it.
- How they will be supported after training.
- Their reporting relationship as a PI Advisor.
- Who to come to for help.

I was surprised to find, at the first one-week training course in December of 1988, that most of the PI Advisors did not really understand what they were getting into. In fact, some said they had not been asked about their interest, but had merely been conscripted. As a result, some of the trainees were neither interested in nor excited about the opportunity. This lack of commitment can be avoided if management takes the time to define and communicate the Advisor's role before sending an employee off to be trained.

Creating a Training and Development Plan

Initially, CPL had no training plan for PI Advisors. Had we started with an overall plan, we would have known what training was available and what was needed for becoming an effective PI Advisor. We pretty well accepted on faith our external consultant's advice that the Advisors needed to attend three weeks of training in process improvement methods. During the first week of training, the Advisors expressed anxiety about their lack of training or experience as instructors and consultants. It did not seem that three weeks of training in process improvement would make us capable of teaching anyone.

Fortunately, this three-week course was scheduled one week per month, which gave us time to voice our concerns to upper management and the external consultant. So we scheduled another week of training in instructional skills. This helped a good bit, and over the summer of 1989, the PI Advisors began to train the organization in process improvement methods.

As teams began to form and work on improving processes, we also found ourselves short on team facilitation skills. To meet this need, the consultant provided our PI Advisors a three-day training course for leaders of PI Teams. Although the course was targeted for team leaders, it was valuable in giving our Advisors a model of how an effective team functions.

Developing Profound Knowledge

Profound knowledge can be defined as the ability to understand why things happen the way they do, and to determine under what conditions the same will happen in the future. This gives us the ability to predict future performance and plan changes that are likely to cause improvement.

New PI Advisors need the opportunity to apply what they have learned before they are rushed into training other people. The challenge for them is to understand the need to learn a little, do a little, then learn and do a little more, on a never-ending cycle of developing profound knowledge. We call it the DeKalb Training Cycle (developed by Larry DeKalb of NuBulk Services), which bears a resemblance to the PDCA Cycle (Figure 6.4):

1. The trainees come with a tremendous amount of experience.
2. Some education takes place, resulting in an increase in knowledge.
3. Some training opportunity lets the trainees apply this knowledge and check how well it works on the job.
4. To the extent that the new knowledge is viewed as useful, it becomes part of their experience.

This learning cycle, which works both in the classroom and in informal coaching, is important. To help others with process improvement, the Advisor must develop experience applying the methods to real work processes.

Eagerly expecting results, CPL managers were impatient for all employees to receive training in process improvement. Responding to this pressure, Advisors in some divisions began training others before they had developed substantial experience. This training con-

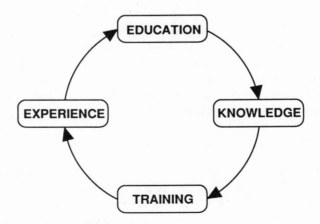

FIGURE 6.4   The DeKalb training cycle.

sisted largely of the Advisor reading the visual aids provided by the consultant, and adding little enthusiasm to the class. Few, if any, improvements resulted from these courses. The participants had not been inspired to use the tools.

In other divisions, the PI Advisors took the time to initiate process improvement efforts in their own areas of responsibility. They formed and led teams in improving such processes as crude oil measurement, expense report processing, and pipeline maintenance. When they began to teach others, they had a wealth of new-found experience to draw upon. Faced with a challenging question, they could explain how they had resolved a similar issue using several of the process improvement methods. This experience made them credible, and participants left the course with the assurance that "if they can do it, so can I!"

Most of the PI Advisors, however, soon found they did not yet have sufficient knowledge and experience to be truly useful to the many teams that were being formed. At this point, in late 1989, we realized that PI Advisors first need to develop profound knowledge in a number of areas:

- *Deming's philosophy of quality improvement.* The Advisor must understand the Fourteen Points, the PDCA Cycle, special and common causes of variation, and how to avoid tampering. We have found that most of a team's "why do it this way" questions can be answered by referring back to these fundamental principles.
- *Process improvement methods and the use of the Seven Basic Tools.* These are the Advisors' basic tools, and their use becomes instinctive over time.
- *Team dynamics and team leadership skills.* Advisors must be able to lead teams and teach them how to work together effectively when they apply process improvement methods. It is amazing how little knowledge most supervisors have in team leadership, and this area was one of our biggest challenges.
- *Presentation and training skills.* Advisors must be able to deliver effective training, which requires a process approach using the PDCA Cycle:
  1. Plan: Develop objectives for each section of training and a course outline to meet these objectives; describe the knowl-

edge to be conveyed; identify a way to measure the knowledge; and establish the level of competence expected.

2. Do: Give the lesson, explain the concept, and provide concrete examples.

3. Check: Have participants perform an activity that requires them to apply the new concept to their previous experience.

4. Act: Move on, provide clarification or special help, depending on how well the participants demonstrate their understanding.

- *Consulting and facilitating skills.* Advisors must develop an understanding of how to manage the process of change. This requires knowledge of human behavior, because TQM means individual change as well as organizational change. There is much resistance to change, and Advisors must be able to size up the status of an individual or team and have an idea of what actions are appropriate.

Evaluating Performance

The Executive Steering Committee is responsible for evaluating and improving the PI Advisor process in the transformation. Likewise, the Local Steering Committee is responsible for evaluating how well the Advisors are functioning in their roles, which are described later in this chapter. None of our Local Steering Committees developed specific criteria to measure the performance of Advisors. Rather, they relied on informal feedback mechanisms, such as communications from supervisors and employees, who know when they have been helped.

This evaluation process resulted in a number of actions:

- During late 1989, it became clear that more Advisors would be needed to provide consulting to as many as a hundred teams throughout CPL. Each Local Steering Committee began selecting and training more Advisors, with an additional seventeen being trained during late 1989 and early 1990.
- By mid-1990, the Executive Steering Committee adopted the three roles of the PI Advisor: Applications Consultant, PIM Instructor, and Internal Consultant.
- The Local Steering Committees then designated the role(s) of

each Advisor. Generally, one Advisor in each division was designated as an Internal Consultant.

- Also during 1990, the Executive Steering Committee recognized substantial variation in how the Local Steering Committees were implementing TQM. We made changes in our external consulting team: one consultant was designated to work with each Local Steering Committee, and all three or four consultants were to meet periodically to improve consistency.

- By late 1990, the Executive Steering Committee decided to focus the efforts of Advisors at the level of natural teams or work groups. At first, Advisors had been invited to all Local Steering Committee meetings. They now stopped participating in these meetings, and the leader of the Local Steering Committee assumed responsibility for coordinating with the Advisors.

- To facilitate the transition of leadership from Advisors to line management, all managers at the Executive and Local Steering Committee levels took one week of Advisor training.

There is another aspect of performance evaluation, however, that deserves attention. An Advisor would sometimes receive a poor performance evaluation from a supervisor in regard to normal job functions, because the Advisor was off doing "quality" work, but not getting any "real" work done. This situation emphasizes the importance of early planning by management. First- and second-line supervisors are put in an unfair position when they lose key personnel, but are expected to continue to perform at the same level. Top management must be willing to commit the resources for the transformation, and must reward quality efforts. People will do what they get rewarded for, and they will certainly avoid performance for which they get punished.

APPLICATIONS CONSULTANT

The first role for all PI Advisors is that of Applications Consultant, helping teams apply process improvement methods. The best place for them to develop this experience is within their own natural work groups.

The time commitment is substantial. At least thirty to fifty percent of the Advisor's time, perhaps more, will be consumed by learning and, later, consulting with teams. As we mature in the TQM transformation, our supervisors will develop the necessary team leadership skills to assume this role.

Responsibilities of the Applications Consultant

There are many types of teams that an Advisor may be responsible for helping. Advisors who are supervisors are the leaders of their natural work teams, which are formed by each first-line supervisor and his or her direct reports. These teams are organizational units: they are not chartered, they already exist. Advisors work with natural teams to help them identify and solve problems in the processes for which they are directly responsible.

Advisors may also become the leaders of Quality Teams (PI Teams), which are chartered by the Executive or Local Steering Committees to address specific issues that are beyond the scope of a natural team. Some Advisors, typically those who function as Internal Consultants, may also consult with Quality Teams.

When working with teams other than their own natural work groups, the Advisor helps to develop and facilitate effective team processes, prepare the leader for his or her role, coach the team in process improvement methods, and provide feedback for improving the team process.

Having to consult with too many teams can tax the time and efforts of Advisors. In our case, the rapid pace of employee training resulted in an explosion of dozens of "classroom teams." Many of these were neither natural teams nor Quality Teams, and some had little or no management support. To reduce the overload, anxiety, and frustration, the Executive Steering Committee decided to focus the Advisors' efforts on natural teams. It also developed a process to charter Quality Teams, so that we did not have more teams than we could support. Beginning with just a few well-managed teams can have more positive impact than having dozens of teams without adequate support.

Selecting Applications Consultants

A prospective Applications Consultant should be:

- Capable of learning and performing this role. This includes communicating effectively with management and co-workers, being a good listener, and having basic math skills (up to basic algebra).

- Respected by co-workers and management, and sought out for advice by peers.
- Interested in the opportunity and in problem solving, and committed to quality improvement.
- An informed risk taker, willing to uncover and communicate problems and seek out opportunities for improvement.

Training Applications Consultants

Before they do any consulting, candidates should have:

- *A thorough understanding of their role.* Talking with their super-visors, managers, and other PI Advisors can help provide this. Our first twelve Advisors had to sort out their roles as training proceeded. By late 1989, these roles had been better defined for training the next seventeen Advisors.
- *Knowledge of TQM philosophy and the organization's philosophy of quality improvement.* Advisors received these fundamentals in a three-day course called "Introduction to the New Management Philosophy," and in discussions with the Local Steering Committees.
- *Knowledge of process improvement methods, statistical problem-solving methods (the Seven Basic Tools), SPC, and concepts of variation.* Advisors received three weeks of training in this area. This training was scheduled one week per month, so they could practice applications back in their own work environment.
- *Training in team dynamics for leading PI Teams.* All Advisors received three days of training in how to lead PI Teams. (This occurred approximately one year after the first Advisors completed the three-week SPC training. Had we planned better, this would have happened sooner.)
- *Facilitator skills.* Advisors received some training in facilitation skills interspersed with the other courses. More knowledge in this area would have been helpful.
- *Additional statistical training as needed.* This may cover subjects such as survey design and design of experiments. Eighteen of our Advisors attended a one-day survey design course in mid-1990.

All of this training was useful to our Advisors, but, as mentioned before, the biggest problem was the pace. Advisors were expected to make the transition from trainee to consultant too rapidly, whereas they really needed more time to develop experience by working with small teams. Also, there was too much early focus on statistical methods, whose value is difficult to explain to a team that is struggling with relationship problems. Moving from autocratic to consensus decision making required more facilitation skills than most of our Advisors possessed.

Working as an Applications Consultant

In our approach to quality improvement, the Advisor's role as an Applications Consultant boils down to this: helping teams and individuals to clarify their purpose, apply process improvement methods, and, in doing so, develop their ability to solve their own problems in the future using a systematic teambuilding approach.

There are no ironclad rules or all-encompassing checklists. The ultimate measure of success is whether the team feels the Advisor has helped. Advisors should be flexible and creative in helping teams, but they need consulting models to help them focus on helping the team. Our external consultant's five-step teambuilding model has been one useful tool in this regard:

1. Assemble the team.
2. Establish team rules.
3. Clarify the team mission.
4. Follow the seven-step problem-solving process.
5. Evaluate and improve the team process.

While we don't always have time to do all of these things, the following list is typical of our Advisors' preparation and facilitation efforts:

- Assess personal bias, remain neutral, and avoid steering the team towards a particular solution. For example, if one is a subject matter expert in the particular area the team is working on, it may prove difficult to remain objective.
- Assess the team's needs and capabilities. This is an informal process of asking questions, listening, and observing the team

process. Some assessment is done before and during the first meeting, but it continues as long as the Advisor works with the team. The Advisor seeks answers to a number of questions:

1. Does the team understand its purpose and how it fits into the process view of the organization?
2. Do the team leader, members, and recorder clearly understand their own roles and that of the PI Advisor?
3. What education and training has the team received in quality philosophy, process improvement methods, problem solving, and the team process?
4. What process does the team use to develop the agenda and record the minutes?
5. Does the team follow ground rules that help them work together effectively?
6. What decision-making processes does the team use, and how effective are they?
7. Is the team working on a problem or implementing a solution? Is it important to all members, and is the scope of the problem within the team's control?
8. What barriers hinder the team from functioning effectively?

- Obtain agreement on the Advisor's role and relationship with the team leader. It goes smoother when the Advisor meets with the leader before the first team meeting to assess the leader's capabilities and needs.

  We have seen problems arise when Advisors just show up at meetings arranged by team leaders. For example, the team leader dominates the meeting, respecting some but disregarding the views of others. In some cases, the Advisor challenges the leader, which only deepens the conflict. In other cases, the Advisor simply observes the process and keeps quiet. The latter is probably the best course, but here the team members may wonder what good the Advisor is doing, and the Advisor loses credibility. Most of us, as Advisors, have learned this lesson the hard way: time spent up front planning with the team leader is a wise investment in the team process.

- Assess the team's abilities and needs during the first team meeting, and refine the Advisor's role with the team. Advisors are clear about roles they will not assume, such as being a team member or the scribe/recorder. Advisors who have been roped into taking notes or participating as a team member have found it very difficult to concentrate on observing and facilitating the team process. Team members must provide the content. Few can handle both roles well.

- Help the team clarify its purpose and objectives when asked to help solve a problem. We often use a round-robin brainstorming session to capture all aspects of a problem, and then help the team define the problem and focus its efforts on identifying the root causes before planning actions.

- Help the team look upstream for root causes if it is stuck on discussing results. We try to ask "why?" five times, although often it doesn't take more than two or three times. We frequently use cause-and-effect diagrams and occasionally interrelationship diagraphs to determine root causes.

- Teach people to think through a process. Ask a series of questions, such as:

  1. What are your outputs? What do you produce or deliver, what services do you provide?

  2. Who are your customers? Who uses your outputs, products, or services?

  3. How do these customers use your outputs?

  4. What are the critical elements of the process that affect how well your output works?

  5. What value do you add?

  At this point, most teams see the value in getting input directly from their customers.

- Focus on the process rather than the content. The Advisor who becomes involved in or takes ownership of the solution becomes part of the problem. The team owns both the problem and the solution.

  Every team deals with both content and process: content is what the team is trying to accomplish, and process is how it goes about doing it. Process is further divided into task and relationship issues. Process task defines how the team goes about managing the content (for example, using an agenda, brainstorming, cause-and-effect diagrams, and so on), and process relationship deals with how people feel along the way.

Our Advisors have found this model useful in keeping their focus on process.

- Help the team develop its own problem-solving abilities. People learn best when they have a real need. Just-in-time training can sometimes be "almost-too-late," but even that is often better than too early.

PROCESS IMPROVEMENT METHODS (PIM) INSTRUCTOR

The PIM Instructor's primary role is to educate and help others learn how to apply process improvement methods.

Responsibilities of a PIM Instructor

PIM Instructors must be able to spend fifty to one-hundred percent of their time away from their primary jobs during training efforts. Their responsibilities are to:

- Continue to work as an Applications Consultant. This experience with teams and facilitating process improvement efforts provides a foundation for teaching others.
- Help the Local Steering Committee and the training coordinator assess training needs and plan courses in the use of process improvement methods.
- Assess the personal needs of trainees and develop their readiness for the course.
- Customize course materials to meet the needs of trainees.
- Involve trainees' supervisors in course delivery and plan how they can support participants after the course.
- Conduct the training course.
- Evaluate how well the training met the trainees' expectations (immediately following the training).
- Help the Local Steering Committee evaluate and improve the training process.

Selecting PIM Instructors

PIM Instructors should be:

- Experienced Applications Consultants with a demonstrated ability to help teams learn process improvement methods.
- Recognized as leaders in process improvement methods, and as role models in the quality approach.
- Interested in educating others, and willing to learn process-based training methods.
- Able to communicate effectively with people at all levels.

Training for PIM Instructors

In addition to the training provided as an Applications Consultant, PIM Instructors need training in adult learning theory and instructional skills. Many of our Advisors had never taught a class and felt like amateurs at first. A five-day course on teaching process improvement methods and developing instructional skills was very valuable for us at this stage.

Working as a PIM Instructor

Instructing employees in the use of simple statistical and problem-solving methods is the primary role of the PIM Instructor. The DeKalb training cycle (Figure 6.4) is an excellent model for applying training methods to effect organizational change. Training must be customized to the trainees' previous experience. Education and transfer of knowledge are possible in the classroom, but turning knowledge into experience happens back on the job.

To be an effective instructor, the readiness of the Advisor and the course material must be considered. Because our Advisors were schedule-driven to become instructors so soon after their own training, many of them relied on the instructional materials provided by our external consultant. Unfortunately, these contained generic examples that had little meaning in the context of our business, and we had not yet had the time to develop our own examples through experience. This lack of preparedness made teaching an uncomfortable experience for many Advisors. More importantly, many participants left the classroom and put the course manual on the shelf next to all the others—to gather dust.

Other Advisors, however, did not encounter these problems to the same extent when they became instructors. It seems they did several things different:

- After being trained, they spent several months leading improvement efforts in work groups and developed solid experience using the new tools.
- They replaced some of the generic examples in the manual with examples from their own experience. This generated credibility and trust.
- They scheduled just one class to teach when they were ready. This class was a pilot session, after which they spent several weeks helping the classroom teams use the tools. This helped the Advisors learn what worked and what did not, so they could make substantive changes to their training approach before scheduling the rest of the classes.

The readiness of the trainees must also be developed before any classroom instruction. Some of our students did not really understand why they were there. Another week away from work to attend some silly class—what a waste of time! They were negative and disruptive during the class, and did not use the tools afterward. They viewed quality as extra work, not their main job. While we had expected some of this attitude, we had not anticipated what a major restraining force it would become. But there were some areas of the company where this problem was easily resolved. The distinguishing feature of these areas was the commitment of managers and supervisors to be role models. For example, the top manager spent up to a day to kick off every class by explaining how Deming's management philosophy does apply to our business. Also, the supervisors were trained before their workers. When enlightened supervisors began to start process improvement efforts in their work groups, the workers wanted to learn more. The supervisors attended the class along with their workers and, in some cases, helped teach them. When natural work groups could sit together at the same classroom table, they began working on relevant problems that they could continue back in the workplace.

When to train is an equally important factor in an instructor's effectiveness. Our Local Steering Committees wanted all employees trained as soon as possible in order to minimize the variation from having both trained and untrained employees. This compelled our Advisors to cover the entire course in one or two sessions. It was not surprising when, long after this training, a team would finally get started and remember very little from the course. Just-in-time training can be more effective, teaching a team the use of a particular tool to address an immediate problem or opportunity at hand.

The experience of participants must be brought into the classroom. Training must be structured, and the instructor should be clear about the purpose and objectives of each element of the course. But the instructor also needs to provide ample opportunity and encouragement for trainees to apply the new knowledge to familiar subject areas.

INTERNAL CONSULTANT

Internal Consultants are those who have developed experience as Applications Consultants and PIM Instructors. They have acquired all the skills needed to address essentially any quality improvement issue.

The role of the Internal Consultant is similar to that of the TQM Coordinator. The TQM Coordinator's scope is the entire company, and he or she reports to the Executive Steering Committee. The Internal Consultant's scope, on the other hand, is defined by the Local Steering Committee to which he or she reports.

Responsibilities of the Internal Consultant

Internal Consultants are likely to spend over fifty percent of their time away from their primary jobs. Much of their time is spent helping the Local Steering Committee learn how to further the TQM transformation. The Advisor must objectively observe the Local Steering Committee process and provide feedback for improvement to the leader and its members. This is challenging, risky, and time-consuming business. Once the Local Steering Committee develops effective feedback and communication systems, this "go between" is no longer needed. As CPL matures as a quality organization, this role will be taken on by managers who have developed the necessary leadership skills.

The Internal Consultant's responsibilities are to:

- Perform applications consulting with their own and other teams.
- Advise local management and help identify and address issues related to the transformation, such as internal barriers to process improvement.
- Consult with Steering Committees, facilitate the use of problem solving, and plan methods to manage and improve the business processes. The Internal Consultant helps Steering Committees charter teams, provides guidance and support, and helps ensure that improvements become standardized.
- Guide other Applications Consultants and PIM Instructors.

Selecting Internal Consultants

Internal Consultants should be experienced as Applications Consultants and PIM Instructors. They must also be able to bring tough issues to the attention of management, and be courageous enough to express unpopular views and see that issues are addressed.

Training for Internal Consultants

Internal Consultants should have completed all the Applications Consultant and PIM Instructor training. Additional training may be useful in subjects such as facilitation skills and the Seven New Management Tools.

Working as an Internal Consultant

The Internal Consultant helps management address many complex issues in the TQM transformation. The nature of this role might be seen in an example from our own experience.

Problem: Although over half of the CPL employees had been trained in process improvement methods, it was clear that they were not using these methods in their daily work. Quality was viewed as extra work.

Approach: In November of 1989, the Executive Steering Committee formed a Quality Planning Team to address the problem. The team included four Steering Committee members (including myself, the Quality Improvement Coordinator), and four external consultants. We followed these steps:

1. The team developed a survey to collect pertinent data throughout CPL.
2. The external consultants visited the home office and each division. They interviewed a cross-section of employees, mostly in focus groups, and recorded all employee comments. Approximately sixteen percent of CPL employees were surveyed.
3. The external consultants met as a team and grouped the qualitative data (employee comments) into common themes using an affinity diagram.
4. The Quality Planning Team reviewed the data. We covered thirty feet of wall with eleven flip charts full of self-stick notes. After a full day, we identified eight key obstacles that contained the essence of the employee input:
   - Roles, relationships, and expectations were not defined, understood, or agreed upon.
   - Support from the external consultants was inadequate.
   - There was a lack of leadership from the Steering Committee.
   - Traditional management behavior was prevalent.
   - Quality improvement methods were not being applied to daily work.
   - Training was inadequate.
   - People were geographically dispersed.
   - Feedback was lacking.
5. The next step was to determine which obstacles to work on and what actions to take. We used an interrelationship diagraph (Figure 6.5) to examine the cause-effect relationship among these multiple issues. We identified three key causes: traditional top-down management behavior, consultant support inadequacies, and geographical dispersion.
   Over several weeks between team meetings, each of us used a systematic diagram to identify actions that could reduce or eliminate the effects of these key causes. At our next meeting,

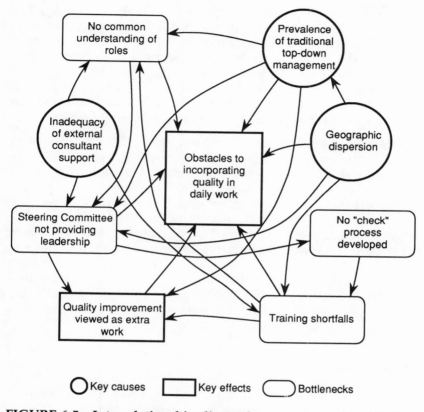

FIGURE 6.5 Interrelationship diagraph.

we identified the primary customers and suppliers of each of the action items, and organized this information in a matrix.

6. We presented this work to the Executive Steering Committee, which used a weighted multi-voting process and a scatter diagram to prioritize the action items.

7. The Quality Planning Team developed a schedule to accomplish the action items. We also developed proposed charters for all the various quality groups, because the lack of understanding of team and individual roles was a key obstacle.

8. The Executive Steering Committee adopted the transformation plan developed by the Quality Planning Team, and re-

named itself the Leadership Steering Team. This was much more than just a name change. Up to this point, the Steering Committee had been primarily involved with learning about quality. Now, the Leadership Steering Team's primary purpose was to establish long-term direction and policy. The Leadership Team developed our vision, mission, and critical success factors, and chartered a Quality Team to integrate our quality philosophy into the business planning process.

These changes have several implications for CPL. A new quality infrastructure emerged: a process view of the company, reflecting the relationship between work processes and the leadership function. This can be depicted as an inverted pyramid. At the top are the natural teams, who perform the work that provides direct services to our customers. The Local Steering Committees, in the middle of the pyramid, provide guidance to the natural teams to optimize the system. The Leadership Steering Team, at the bottom of the pyramid, provides overall CPL vision and leadership. Also, a new form of leadership began to take root, and a new business planning process became the driver for integrating quality concepts into our many business systems. Quality and business would no longer function as two separate parallel structures.

SUMMARY

Selecting and developing capable people to become PI Advisors is an important part of the change process. Before selecting Advisors, top management must develop a clear understanding of their purpose and roles in implementing TQM. Management must support the Advisors. After developing extensive knowledge and experience, the Advisors provide training and applications consulting to all employees. This is a major factor in empowering employees with the knowledge and resources they need, so that they can take ownership for continuously improving the way work gets done.

CPL is now well into the fourth year of the transformation, and PI Advisors continue to play a crucial role. All across the company, supervisors are trying and learning to adopt the new philosophy in their role as natural team leaders. They need the PI Advisors now more than ever. Supervisors understand that they must develop the skills to be PI Advisors for their natural teams. And management understands that change is a long-term process.

7

The Process
Improvement Team

TRAINING AND EDUCATION DEPARTMENT
H. M. Smyth Company
AND
DAWN L. SORENSON

Process Improvement (PI) Teams are established to work on any process or problem—technical or cultural—that is vital to the organization's mission. Most teams are chartered by Local Steering Committees and consist of employees who are trained in SPC and team effectiveness (Figure 7.1), but team membership depends highly on the particular process being studied. Management should champion any team that is chartered and periodically assess the need for management support. The organization may have many or few teams operating at any one time, but each team should be kept as small as possible. Ideally, teams should include:

• People who work in the process.
• Customers of the process.
• Suppliers to the process.
• The supervisor of the process.
• A facilitator as required.

The PI Team's major responsibilities are to:

• Clearly define the process or problem.

101

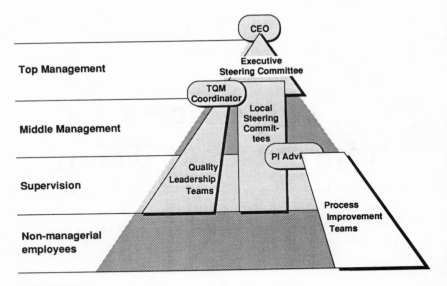

FIGURE 7.1

- Establish how the problem relates to the organization's mission and objectives.
- Establish ground rules and administrative procedures.
- Ensure that the right people are selected to address the problem or process.
- Coordinate and communicate regularly with the Steering Committee that is directly responsible for the process.
- Recommend changes to the process or steps to resolve the problem, based on appropriate data analysis.
- Periodically assess progress and conformance to the team's mission, objectives, and ground rules.

This chapter describes the team model used at H. M. Smyth Company, Inc.

PROFILE: H. M. SMYTH COMPANY

Tapping the creative resource that exists in every worker is a key to the challenges that face American industry in our changing world.

The structure of Process Improvement (PI) Teams provides a channel for this resource. At the H. M. Smyth Company, teamwork has been a major component in the quality transformation process.

H. M. Smyth Company began operations as a commercial printer in 1877, and has played a major role in Minnesota's printing industry. In the late 1950s, the company began to shape itself around the area of label specialization, marketing aggressively to label users in many industries. Today, eighty-five percent of the firm's annual sales volume is represented by label production for industries such as food processing, beverages, industrial and manufacturing, toys and recreation, medical products, toiletries, cosmetics, personal care, and paint manufacturing. Smyth has worked closely with some of Minnesota's largest corporations, and has become a nationally recognized label producer. Of the company's list of top twenty-five customers, seventeen are Fortune 500 companies.

In the late 1970s, Smyth's executive management saw the pressure that the foreign market was exerting on American industry. Many of the company's customers were entering into quality programs, which indicated the need for Smyth, as their supplier, to keep pace or lose them to aggressive foreign competition.

OUR PATH TO TRANSFORMATION

The quality of our printed products had always been a major focus for the employees. For the most part, employees had a great deal of pride and confidence in their work. The company had realized steady growth in the customer base and worked hard to develop strong relationships with all customers, both large and small.

Despite this strong culture of customer service, it seemed that our problems were always of the same nature. Customer requirements were not always filled satisfactorily, and there was no concentrated effort to prevent those problems from recurring. Weekly management meetings were often a rehash of the previous week's mistakes, and it became clear that asking managers to identify the source of a problem after the fact was not effective in *preventing* a problem from happening in the first place.

The president, who was the leader of these management meetings, recognized that a more positive way of dealing with the world at Smyth had to be introduced. He began distributing books to the managers with assigned reading and discussion objectives. Blanchard's *One Minute Manager* (1982) series, Iacocca's autobiography (1986), Peters' *In Search of Excellence* (1982), and others, became discussion topics. In less than a year, the climate of the meetings improved, but the same production problems kept reappearing.

Responding to the advice of a customer, the executive managers attended a Deming seminar in August of 1987. The four-day session created great excitement and enthusiasm as it tied together many of the ideas that had already been tried. The Deming seminar provided much more than a list of action items: it showed that fundamental changes were needed in management philosophy. Riding on this wave of excitement, executive management attempted to implement these changes for the next six months—but with only minor success.

Determined to do it right, executive management formed a Steering Committee consisting of representatives from each department, including both employees and managers. As the process improvement efforts intensified, the Steering Committee was restructured to include only the CEO and his direct reports, in order to focus the responsibility of the transformation directly on those at the top. The Steering Committee decided to seek the expertise of an outside consultant to help identify the best method of bringing the new philosophy to Smyth. Three firms submitted proposals, and in May of 1988, we selected our consultant, based on the consultant's familiarity with Dr. Deming's philosophy and ability to work with a union manufacturing firm.

One of the consultant's first steps was to conduct a needs assessment to determine the strengths and weaknesses of the organization and how the consultant could best assist our quality improvement efforts. The results of the needs assessment showed that the company possessed many strengths: loyal employees, good working conditions, and continued growth. The needs assessment also identified areas needing attention: communication, teamwork, and empowered employees.

These results were not really a surprise to employees. Management had often encouraged competition rather than cooperation, and, traditionally, production employees were encouraged to leave their brains at the door. Based on the new philosophy, employees were now being encouraged to solve their own problems with support and coaching from management. It was important to address those areas where employees could see the commitment of top management.

The consultant assisted the Steering Committee in mapping out a plan for these concerns. As part of this plan, executive management randomly selected thirty-five additional employees to attend a Deming seminar to broaden the base of awareness within the company. These employees were from all levels of the company, but the majority were managers and line supervisors who would help bring awareness of the transformation to the grass-roots level. After this training, four subcommittees were formed from the original Steering Committee to provide direction for strategic planning, training and education, employee involvement, and process improvement.

TEAM TRAINING

Although we recognized the importance of teams for process improvement and the objectives they served, we were uncertain about the actual steps to building teams. We searched for information, but found little on how to structure meetings, select team roles, and establish a focus. Each time teambuilding had been taught, the results were the same: the supervisor held a departmental meeting to discuss the importance of teams, and the employees generated lists of problems that needed fixing. The supervisor was left with a frustrating itemization of everything that was wrong, and the employees walked away feeling that nothing was really going to change no matter how good the effort. Functioning as a team was an admirable idea, but how, exactly, did this happen in the workplace?

The employees were used to working in a more controlled environment built on a traditional style of management. Although there were some departments and informal groups that appeared to work as cohesive units, focused teamwork was something that happened mostly by accident. Identifying and mastering teambuilding skills would require structure and training. Management and employees alike had much to learn about the behavior that would transform Smyth from a group of individuals into a cohesive team capable of realizing the company's vision.

All four subcommittees that were directing our efforts agreed that for the program to be successful, every employee would need some training in quality, job skills, and personal development. The training and education department, along with five middle managers who had been through the consultant's SPC series, prepared a training program consisting of seven modules.

1. *Team development*. Establish a decision-making process, select a leader, establish ground rules, and clarify the mission or purpose of the team.
2. *Understanding the process*. Those involved in the process flow-chart the process, and identify the customer-supplier relationships that exist internally and externally to the process.
3. *Brainstorming*. Isolate target areas for improvement through the use of cause-and-effect diagrams, Pareto charts, and correlation charts.
4. *Developing process data*. Determine the appropriate data to gather, identify appropriate tools for measurement and data gathering, and collect the data.
5. *Data analysis*. Analyze the data through the use of histograms, run charts, and control charts.
6. *System analysis*. Determine the stability and capability of the process.
7. *Process improvement*. Apply all the preceding methods to identify process improvement, decide on a small test case, implement a change, check the results, and determine whether a permanent change to the process is applicable. These methods of process improvement are applications of the PDCA Cycle.

This training was concurrent with employees participating on teams through a project formed by the process improvement sub-committee. The project was designed to reduce the company's number one waste problem: paper. The intent was to train the employees in SPC and have them immediately apply their learning to process improvement. Executive management made a commitment that team members be allotted two hours per week for training and team involvement—five percent of their work week.

The project started with an overview of Deming's Fourteen Points and the Smyth Path to Transformation, which described the process the company went through and the groundwork that was laid before the introduction of PI Teams (Figure 7.2).

The employees were also invited to volunteer for a team. Sixty-three of the 185 employees accepted the invitation, which we considered a positive sign. If one looks at a normal bell-shaped curve (Figure 7.3), one can see how employees enter the transformation process in six general categories:

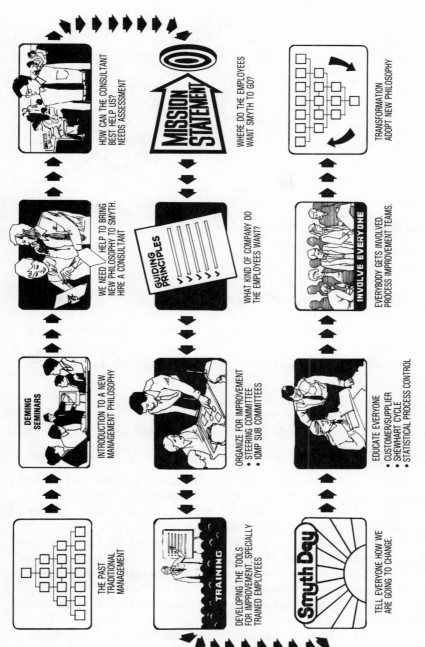

FIGURE 7.2 Smyth's path to transformation.

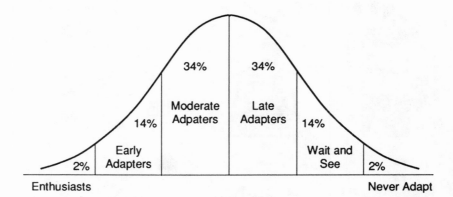

FIGURE 7.3   Employee adaptation to change.

1. Enthusiasts (two percent of the employees) take a leadership role in the change process.
2. Early adapters (fourteen percent) adapt to change early in the program.
3. Moderate adapters (thirty-four percent) need some convincing.
4. Late adapters (thirty-four percent) wait to see if change is serious.
5. Wait-and-see employees (fourteen percent) hold back until they see if change will work.
6. Never-adapt employees (two percent) will never adapt to the change.

By this measure, our sixty-three volunteers showed that we had built a critical mass of thirty-four percent among our employees, and that we had already involved the enthusiasts, the early adapters, and about half of the moderate adapters.

The volunteers were broken into groups of six, and they attended weekly two-hour training sessions for eleven weeks. At the end of the eleven-week project, executive management evaluated its effectiveness. The evidence indicated that the tools of SPC were indeed applicable, but that actual improvements by the teams were minimal.

We revised the SPC training to provide education prior to team participation. This was a more successful approach, because it helped trainees understand the tools before they were expected to use them in a team. A concentrated effort was then made to train every employee in SPC, which was completed in mid-1990.

The teams that had been trained during the paper-waste project were reorganized to involve only those employees who had a direct impact on paper waste. One of the teams was a group of four pressmen working on feeder setup for the press. They developed the following mission statement:

> Our mission is to develop a standard procedure for setting up and running the feeder. By setting up this standard procedure we will reduce the number of knock-offs and thereby reduce paper and time waste which will increase productivity and profit.

This team met once a week for an hour over the next seven months. They charted their process, collected data, and reached their objective of developing a standard operating procedure. To prove the effectiveness of their procedure, they continued to collect data and realized a fifty percent reduction in the number of knock-offs per hour on the press. (A knock-off occurs when sheets are not fed through the press properly, resulting in a press shutdown and paper pile-up.)

SELECTING AND DEVELOPING TEAM MEMBERS

Our experience with building teams has provided us with several guidelines for successfully selecting and developing teams.

Selecting Members

Presently, our teams are selected by middle management from those employees who have expressed a desire to participate. Selection is based on three criteria:

1. *Do they work in the process?* One of the teams working on paper waste directed its efforts toward the process of make-ready (setting up). All members from the team were involved in the make-ready process.
2. *Are they suppliers to the process?* Another team had members

from both the customer service and shipping departments, because customer service supplied information to shipping.

3. *Are they customers to the process?* To collect data on waste in the press department due to product defects, a bindery employee was asked to be on the team, because the bindery is the internal customer of the press department.

Potential team members are selected and then reviewed by the project facilitator. This review, which determines the qualifications and capabilities of each team member, is based on knowledge, skills, and attitude:

Knowledge. Knowledge refers to prerequisite education requirements:

- *Basic SPC tools.* The use of statistics is essential for process improvement. Each member of a team must understand the basic statistical tools and how to use them. SPC training was provided through an internally developed program and taught by those individuals who had originally been through the consultant's training program.
- *Team development.* Team members are taught the essentials of conducting an effective team meeting. They learn how to assign responsibilities, reach decisions by consensus, and write a mission statement that identifies their objectives.
- *Continuous process improvement.* To continually improve, the team members must have a clear understanding of the PDCA Cycle:
  Plan—Define the opportunity and plan the change.
  Do—Test the change on a small scale.
  Check—Measure the effectiveness of the change.
  Act—Make the change a standard procedure within the process.

Skills. Interaction skills may be inherent or learned. They include:

- *Personal profile.* The effectiveness of teamwork is largely determined by the profile of its members. Everyone has a distinct preference about how to solve problems, interact with others, and accomplish assigned tasks. To function in a team setting, each person must understand his or her own profile and value the differences in other members. The Personal Profile, which we developed from a number of psychology source books, is an information sheet filled out by all team members to help identify their preferences for working, communicating, and problem solving.

- *Communication.* Team members are taught how to listen and effectively communicate ideas. This training is done in relationship to the Personal Profile, which develops a consciousness of how the team members affect each other. This helps avoid the conflict, confusion, and mistrust that is common to many teams.

- *Negotiation (presentation style).* The ultimate responsibility for changing processes and systems rests on the shoulders of all management. Teams invest a great deal of energy gathering information and collecting and charting data, and it is important that they communicate their findings effectively in order to negotiate change. To that end, each member is taught how to use statistics in making presentations.

Attitude. The attitude and behavior of team members are important factors in any project.

- *Enthusiasm.* Although enthusiasm leaves room for subjective selection of a team member, it is important that participants show some signs of enthusiasm.

- *Willingness.* The potential team member must be willing to work on the problem statement. Sometimes employees may be enthusiastic to activate change but have no desire to focus on the assigned problem.

- *Commitment.* Every member must understand that becoming a team participant requires a commitment of time, energy, and the dedication to work at the assigned task until satisfactory completion.

Participation on a team without proper training may result in the entire team becoming sidetracked by improper procedures. Volunteers who do not meet the educational requirements are scheduled into the respective educational program by the training and education department.

Assigning Responsibilities

When team members are selected, they begin by identifying their roles and responsibilities.

Team Members

Teams consist of those employees who have a direct impact on the project. Team members commit to team participation until the project is complete. Their responsibilities are to:

- Attend all team meetings and be on time.
- Listen and be considerate of other team members, valuing the differences of each.
- Limit criticism to ideas, not people.
- Assume assignments and carry them out—on time.
- Cooperate to reach consensus decisions.
- Avoid bringing hidden agendas to the meeting.

Team Leader

The team selects a leader through consensus decision making. The leader must understand the process and focus of the team, as well as the importance of each team member's profile, striving toward synergy for the successful completion of the project. The leader's responsibilities are to:

- Prepare an agenda. The agenda serves to keep the meeting on track, eliminate side-bar conversations, and helps the leader begin and end meetings on time. The agenda should include the action register from the previous meeting and the meeting objectives based on the team function flowchart for process improvement.
- Schedule the meeting time and place, and reserve the meeting room in advance of the meeting. Team meetings should be held the same day and time each week so that it becomes a matter of routine for members (and easier to reserve meeting rooms). Meetings should be held in a quiet area where there will be no interruptions.

- Notify the switchboard operator of the meeting time, place, and participants, so all calls can be held, avoiding interruptions.
- Keep the team and the discussion on track, thus keeping the mission in focus.
- Encourage everyone's participation.

Team Recorder

The recorder is a position that rotates among the team members. (We rotate in alphabetical order.) The recorder's responsibilities are to:

- Fill out the meeting form, recording the time, date, members present, and the action register items.
- Collect a copy of all data charting.
- Record meeting activities.
- Provide a copy of the minutes and the action register to all participants and the project facilitator at the end of each meeting.

These functions ensure that by the end of every team meeting, all members will know their responsibilities and assignments for the next meeting. Assignments should be distributed evenly among all members, and they must be documented in an action register.

Developing a Mission Statement

The mission statement is the second item on a team's agenda. This is a very important part of the planning stage for a project, because it takes the team through the process of defining the team's goal. A mission statement addresses three issues:

1. *What is the goal of the team?* The statement should be written in terms that every team member can understand and agree upon. This goal, when put in writing, helps the team focus on a target and strengthens the commitment of each member.
2. *Why is the goal important?* This justifies the goal and clarifies the reason for focusing on the defined target. The "why" takes

into consideration the stakeholders of the project, which may include internal and external customers.

3. *How will the goal be reached?* The strategy explains the tools and vehicles that the team will use in reaching their goal.

When these three issues are addressed in forming the team's mission statement, it serves as a guide and road map for the project, helping the team to stay motivated and on track. The team members then proceed through the PDCA Cycle until they have reached their objective (mission).

Evaluating Progress

The main responsibility for evaluating teams rests with the Steering Committee, but teams are encouraged to evaluate their own progress consistently in two specific areas: team process and purpose fulfillment. Team process can be evaluated by considering how well the team made decisions, communicated openly, followed ground rules, met regularly, and so on. Purpose fulfillment can be evaluated by considering how well the team worked toward achieving its mission, planned its activities, and used SPC tools. Periodically evaluating both areas can identify potential problems and help the group realize success more quickly.

Team evaluations take place at the end of each team meeting. A short period of time is set aside for self-evaluation and discussion of how well the objectives were met. Did they understand all the concepts introduced at the meeting? In which areas do they need additional help to meet their goal? What are their comments on team dynamics, adherence to ground rules, training format, and ideas for improvement? Any problems identified by the team, the training department, or the Steering Committee, can be worked on immediately. This regular self-evaluation also serves to keep the team on task and prevents more time-consuming evaluations later in the process.

Management Support

To lay the groundwork for teams, management must understand the need for and process of teambuilding, and communicate absolute commitment to it. Management's understanding and commitment are important because employees need to see congruency between management's words and actions. Without this, the job of total change is far more difficult. For example, if a manager agrees to the importance of teamwork, it is essential that he or she provide the time and coverage for employees to meet as a team during regular work hours. Otherwise, confusion ensues about what is really important: working as a team or putting out fires? Management must continually monitor its actions and words, so that the message to employees is consistent and focused.

Building effective PI Teams and empowering them to improve the quality of goods and services are thus the responsibilities of top management. Teams can be started at any time, but to ensure their effectiveness, management must:

- Be educated.
- Be supportive.
- Provide a focus for teams, such as education, process improvement, or a specific project.
- Be committed for the long haul.

It is also management's responsibility and obligation to provide the needed support in a way that doesn't stifle the team's creativity. For example, in developing a mission statement, the team will often look to the Steering Committee and other members of management for guidance. One particular team created a mission statement that was entirely too broad to achieve successfully: "The mission of the paper yield layout team is to reduce paper waste." Management suggested that the team consider not only what their purpose was, but how they would accomplish that task. At this stage, it was crucial that management coach the team, motivating its members to keep working on the mission statement and making them feel valued in their work.

It is absolutely critical that all management levels understand and commit to TQM. This knowledge must encompass all management activities and processes, so that managers know how to support their people, as well as understanding how manufacturing processes are improved. This support includes regularly communicating corporate plans, giving feedback, and ensuring that all employees have the time and resources for their team activities.

SUMMARY

Our paper-waste project served as a company-wide introduction to the use of statistical tools, and the employees who had been involved in it went on to become the motivators for new teams and process improvement efforts. During our initial project, the hidden entrepreneurship of the PI Team members surfaced to produce amazing results.

The project lasted eleven months. In the first six months, the estimated investment for training was $45,000, including lost production time. In the same six-month period, the company realized a savings of $118,000 due to paper-waste reduction. This $118,000 represents a 162 percent return on investment. The benefits, however, are far more than dollars and cents.

A generation of employees who had been indoctrinated to be lone rangers are now cooperating as a team. Communication that once was stopped by barriers between departments is now more free-flowing and less frustrating. The entire company now speaks a new language—the language of statistics. Even the simplest of questions these days may be answered, "I don't know, let's check the data."

Smyth cannot boast of having arrived, because the road is certainly long. As Dr. Deming reminds us, process improvement is not a project but a process that never ends. The H. M. Smyth Company has accepted this challenge of never-ending improvement. As problems arise, new teams will be formed to solve them. The road may be long, but the newly established benchmarks prove that it is the right direction.

8

The Consultant

JOHN PERSICO, JR., AND SHARON K. LOUBERT
Process Management International

The external consultant's role in a TQM effort is to provide developmental resources not readily available within the organization. The consultant works with the client to create and develop processes and structures that will build the impelling forces of change and ensure that the restraining forces do not overcome the effort. Most TQM efforts require consulting expertise in two areas: 1) statistics and process improvement; and 2) training, organizational development, and industrial relations.

The external consultants work closely with the organization's designated internal consultants, so that a transfer of knowledge takes place. This helps ensure that at some point the organization will be able to continue the transformation on its own and not be forever dependent on the skills and services of external consultants.

The consultants' major responsibilities are to:

- Understand the client's business and culture.
- Establish the leadership for the TQM effort.
- Formalize working procedures and establish mutual expectations with the TQM Coordinator, the Executive Steering Committee, and union leadership (when appropriate).
- Develop a tentative road map for the first year with the Executive Steering Committee and the TQM Coordinator.
- Educate and train management and union leadership in transformation concepts and process management.

117

- Facilitate the Executive Steering Committee and other teams, and oversee the development of team skills.
- Work with the Executive Steering Committee to align the organization's mission and values with the goals of the TQM effort.
- Identify and prepare in-house teams and PI Advisors for the effort.
- Assist with the initial improvement projects.
- Help the Executive Steering Committee regularly diagnose the TQM effort.

This chapter describes the roles and methodologies of the consultants at PMI.

WHY A CONSULTANT?

Our transformation model calls for consulting expertise in both statistics and human resources development. This is consistent with the socio-technical approach that views organizations as composed of two dominant systems (Pasmore 1988). The social system includes such issues as employee policies, procedures, work rules, norms, culture, work incentives, and quality of worklife. The technical system includes the machines, materials, work processes, and technology that are directly responsible for the final product or service. Only by addressing both systems can an organization make an effective transformation. Since it is difficult to find one consultant with enough expertise in both these areas, PMI assigns two consultants in a TQM effort to work together:

- The Process Improvement (PI) consultant provides skills in statistics and statistical process control (SPC), helping to establish the goals and directions for a change in the technical system.
- The Organizational Development (OD) consultant offers a broad background in human resource development, training, organizational development, and industrial relations, helping to establish a change in the social system.

In addition to these areas of expertise, both consultants should be competent in basic consulting skills: rapport-building, diagnostic, influence, and administrative and managerial skills (Spencer and Cullen 1981).

Working together, the two consultants play an essential role in the TQM effort, but this role can be difficult when the client's expectations are unclear. The "mystique" of a consultant is aggravated by the fact that many organizations have little or no experience with consultants, while others have developed negative stereotypes from their experiences. Furthermore, consultants too often assume that the client understands why they are needed. In most cases, this assumption is unwarranted.

Turner (1982) identifies a hierarchy of purposes for a consultant: providing information, providing solutions, making a diagnosis, making recommendations, assisting with implementation, building a consensus, facilitating learning, and improving organizational effectiveness. Despite this seemingly comprehensive list, some may still argue that the question remains: "Why do I need a consultant? Why hire an outside person?" There are several answers to this question, but some can be difficult to admit:

- An external consultant provides a knowledge of quality theory and a breadth of experience not available within the organization.

- Improvement requires the ability to view an organization objectively and point out problems that no one either notices or wants to hear. This can be difficult, even career-threatening for an employee. External consultants have more leverage as neutral parties, since they are not tied into roles and responsibilities that limit challenging the system.

- Management may attempt to delegate quality improvement. An external consultant should not assume that responsibility, and instead will work to see that management takes ownership of the effort.

- The external consultant must be able to work with all levels of employees, while the internal consultant is often viewed as a subordinate by senior management.

- The organization cannot afford to wait until they have trained someone.

- A consultant's time can be allocated more flexibly than that of a full-time employee. The consultant can also be viewed as a temporary expediency due to the "project" nature of the effort, and can generally be terminated at any time.

- The organization has limited time to put into developmental activities and would rather hire someone on an as-needed basis.

A more fundamental answer to the question of hiring a consultant can be seen in how companies are often organized for growth, not development. While most organizations have departments for production, sales, marketing, and maintenance, fewer have human resource, training, or research and development departments. Even fewer have departments of leadership, communication, or education. The simple fact is that few organizations do a good job of balancing their needs: the usual focus on growth generally means a lack of resources for development.

There are also some potential drawbacks to hiring a consultant. The major disadvantages are in the areas of resource allocation, credibility, and rapport.

- *Resource allocation.* Despite the hyperbole of most consultants' claims that the project will pay for itself, an organization has no guarantee of this. The time and money allocated to consultant-related activities may not be part of the organization's ongoing priorities, and consultant activities may directly compete with the resources needed to sustain the organization in the short term. No consultant can or should guarantee a return on investment. First, no two organizations are alike, and a consultant's success with one organization cannot guarantee success with another. Second, there are many variables affecting the success of an effort that are beyond the consultant's control. The consultant should help the client understand what the effort will involve, and together they should establish guidelines for mutual responsibility of the effort.
- *Credibility.* The organization should have clear expectations about the consultant's role and responsibilities, and this role must be accepted by management and all those with whom the consultant will be working. At the same time, the consultant must develop a basic understanding of the client's core business. No matter how much expertise a consultant may have in any one area, the consultant will be less effective without the "big picture" of the organization.

- *Rapport.* Consultant-client rapport is essential. This does not mean that the consultant and the client must become close friends. It does mean that the consultant must be honest, knowledgeable, ethical, trustworthy, and have the client's interests above his or her own gain. The more the consultant cares about the organization, and the more the client believes this, the more likely the consultant will be successful.

THE ORGANIZATIONAL DEVELOPMENT (OD) CONSULTANT

Objectives

The major objectives of the OD consultant are to help the organization develop its own resources, and to enlist these resources in the transformation. These objectives may be thought of in terms of force field analysis (Lewin 1952). In every organization there are forces that either help or retard moving toward more productive behavior. The consultant must identify these forces and build a strategy for addressing them during the TQM effort. They can be categorized as impelling and restraining forces:

Impelling Forces	*Restraining Forces*
• Leadership	• Unrealistic expectations
• Training and education	• Inadequate skills
• Constancy of purpose	• Failure to follow through
• Long-term vision and planning	• Management unwillingness to role-model new behaviors and skills
• Pride of work	
• Environment conducive to creativity and risk-taking	• Management, labor, or union resistance
	• Inadequate support

Consultants cannot hope to overcome the restraining forces in an organization by sheer force. They must build up the impelling forces through education and training, while simultaneously changing the systems and processes that support the restraining forces. This cannot be done overnight. It requires a collaborative effort of both external and internal consultants to see that systems are put into place that can address such long-range goals.

A Model for Change

No two organizations are alike. We asked one client whether examples from another, similar company that was pursuing TQM would help them. The response was, "No, we're very different." It is common to hear clients say that something won't work here because "we are different," and paradoxically that "we don't want to reinvent the wheel." A model is essential to help answer this need for flexibility while also providing some structure.

Fundamental differences in structure, purpose, and systems, mean that the consultants must have a model or change strategy that can be adapted to these nuances. At the same time, the model can be used to formulate hypotheses, test assumptions, and validate expectations about what will and should happen during the TQM effort. The PMI transformation model provides stability in dealing with organizations from a broad array of industries. As described in the Introduction, there are four basic stages in this model: planning, education, implementation, and continuous improvement. Both the OD and PI consultants help the organization work through these stages, developing its ability to continue to negotiate them on its own.

The Planning Phase

In the planning stage, both consultants work to:

- Understand the organization's business and culture.
- Establish the leadership for the effort.
- Establish mutual expectations.
- Formalize working procedures.
- Identify first priorities for the effort.
- Develop a tentative road map for the first year.

Understand the Client's Business and Culture

The consultant's first responsibility is to understand the client's business, problems, goals, ideals, and culture. The OD consultant relies on a variety of tools and resources, such as written materials, focus groups, interviews, and questionnaires to foster this understanding.

For example, we worked with a company that produced paper rolls for the printing industry. Even before meeting with management, we conducted a literature review and asked to see any customer or employee surveys they had conducted over the last few years. This provided both the OD and PI consultants with a much better understanding of the paper industry, as well as a detailed understanding of the company's problems, concerns, culture, and personality.

Establish the Leadership for the Effort

The OD consultant must identify the power structure in the organization and help establish the group of leaders who will be coordinating the system-wide TQM changes. The roles and responsibilities of all the leaders must be clearly defined.

Sometimes this is done in private sessions and discussions with the CEO. At a company that manufactures generator sets for recreation and industry, the OD consultant met for several months with the CEO and a senior vice president to discuss the scope and responsibilities of the major parties who would be involved in the TQM effort. These sessions provided the company a better understanding of the resources required to implement TQM, which helped them plan the effort and decide on priorities.

The role of union leadership in the effort must also be established at this time. Many managers do not realize that for TQM to be successful, union leadership must be involved as full partners in the effort. It cannot be just token involvement. Too often the union–management relationship is adversarial or confrontational, and management will tell us, "There is no way we'll sit down together with the union!" Not surprisingly, we hear much the same from union leadership: "No way will we work with management!" Union leadership is often afraid that cooperation will be mistaken for being co-opted, that is, "getting in bed" with management.

Thus, in a union environment, one of the key roles of the OD consultant is to begin helping the union and management work together, demonstrating to both sides that this will be a win–win effort. Even more important, both sides must understand what the wins will be and what's in it for them to sit down together in a collaborative relationship.

Establish Mutual Expectations

Clients sometimes assume that they know what is needed and how the consultants should operate. These assumptions seldom match reality. The OD consultant must identify the expectations and assumptions on both sides so that contradictory or incompatible objectives can be resolved. This can be done through interviews or as part of a structured exercise on setting expectations.

In the case of a company that makes eyeglasses, our initial relationship was established during a question-and-answer session with a senior vice president. Among the expectation-setting questions we asked were: What do you dislike most about consultants? What are the sacred cows in the organization? What will you need to do differently if this effort is going to be successful? The executive expressed his surprise at our candidness and our willingness to accept criticism and listen to his concerns. This openness and trust helped get us off to a good start with an important leader in the organization.

Formalize Working Procedures

Both the client's and the consultant's preferences and business requirements place certain limitations on the TQM effort. Overall budget and time allocations are important issues to negotiate. These nuts-and-bolts issues must be addressed as early as possible in the planning stage, and the agreements may be formalized with a written contract.

Identify First Priorities for the Effort

First efforts must be developed around meaningful and manageable objectives. The scope of the project must be focused on starting points and priorities that will create a beachhead for further expansion and success of the TQM effort. It is critical that first efforts are well planned and implemented in areas with a high likelihood of success.

Develop a Tentative Road Map for the First Year

Both consultants must work with senior management to develop a tentative road map, which is the culmination of the first wave of planning. This is much like developing a computer program, where a programmer (the consultant) and a subject matter expert (the client) are paired together. This road map is both educational and functional. It provides an overview of where the effort is headed and, more pragmatically, allows the organization and the consultants to jointly plan upcoming events, training, consulting, client responsibilities, and the priority and sequence of the first year's activities. At this early stage, the road map is at best a rough approximation of what they would like to have happen during the first year, and it will need to be revised and clarified as the effort proceeds. At one large healthcare corporation, it took nearly a year to develop the road map due to a false start when the organization embarked on TQM without involving the unions that represented major groups of professionals.

An example of a road map is shown in Figure 8.1, which focuses specifically on the planning process for Quality Leadership Teams. It is actually an integrated flowchart that shows the various groups and people who need to be involved and the approximate order of the first year's events. Many different formats—Gantt charts, PERT charts, tree diagrams—can be used to depict the people, events, time, and interrelationships with a realistic level of complexity.

The Education Phase

Training and consulting are partners in the change effort. In the education phase, formal training needs are assessed and implemented. During this phase, the objectives of both the OD and PI consultants are to:

- Assess educational needs and training plans.
- Develop a common language and understanding of quality improvement concepts and methodologies.
- Educate the client in transformation concepts and methods.
- Identify and prepare in-house leaders in the effort.

Assess Educational Needs

The OD and PI consultants work together to assess and provide training for the organization. The OD consultant identifies the skills that are needed in presentation, facilitation, team effectiveness, and TQM concepts. Training and education may go beyond the formal

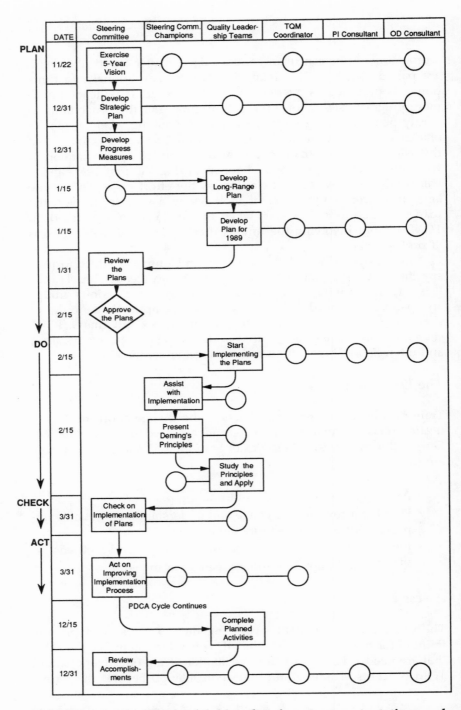

FIGURE 8.1 Quality leadership planning process: tentative road maps.

classroom setting. The OD consultant may work with management to design a program of readings, seminars, company visits, telephone calls, videos, and so on.

The process of education is very evident in the early stages of TQM, but a long-range plan for the continuing education and development of all employees must be developed. At a small printing company, a task force put together a training plan that had three basic elements: technical training for the job, quality training (including statistics and other process improvement tools), and human relations training (leadership, communication, and teambuilding skills).

Studies show that many American companies allocate less than 1 percent of payroll on training, while "world-class" companies such as Xerox and Motorola spend nearly 5 percent. At some point in the process, it is necessary to put hard dollars into training and to develop a plan for keeping these dollars focused on training. Although training departments often become mini-bureaucracies that ignore the real needs of the organization, it is also true that training budgets are too often cut back when times are rough, which may be just when training is needed the most.

Develop a Common Language

TQM methodology comes with a unique vocabulary that soon distinguishes those trained in TQM from those not trained. Both consultants promote this vocabulary, because it is a powerful tool in unifying the organization and breaking down boundaries. Because it may also alienate some members, the consultant must be willing to adapt the vocabulary to each organization. The important point is not to dwell on what things are called, but to develop a common vocabulary.

Educate the Client in Transformation Concepts and Methods

The more the client understands the process and objectives of TQM, the more realistic expectations will be. Clients may resist this understanding for a variety of reasons. Some clients are not willing to devote the time to understand. Others have difficulty understanding organizational transformation concepts, of which many are admittedly not well defined. Finally, many clients are more results-oriented than process-oriented: they do not want to know how the process works, but only when it will produce the desired objectives.

A manager once complained that he preferred to have to do less reading and would appreciate it if I could just give him the "facts." I asked him if he would tell his exercise coach that he wanted the coach to do the exercises for him and save him the effort. Busy managers do not typically have much time for reading or other creative activities, and so it is often best to use many different vehicles for educating them in the fundamentals of TQM. We often encourage them to attend conferences and to call or meet with other clients to discuss common concerns. Nevertheless, there is still a good deal of reading and formal education that is needed.

The more the client understands organizational transformation, the more likely the client will be able to help the consultant design and implement ways to overcome roadblocks. The process then becomes one of mutual responsibility and cooperative teamwork. When this happens, it is no longer the consultant's program, and the client may now be said to be mature. The client is more realistic about expectations of progress and what the consultant can do. This is a significant milestone in the education phase.

Identify and Prepare In-House Leaders in the Effort

The primary purpose of both the PI and OD consultants is to enable the organization to acquire the ability to provide for its own development. Both consultants help identify capable individuals to be trained as PI Advisors, who become the organization's internal technical consultants. These people must be positioned to take maximum advantage of their strengths in the TQM effort.

We have been working with Inco-Manitoba on and off for over five years. Officially, the relationship ended after the second year, but the OD consultant is often called upon for advice or help as issues come up. The company knows, however, that they cannot transfer the work to the external consultant, and that they are ultimately responsible for the success of their effort.

The Implementation Phase

The implementation phase sees the beginning of efforts to attack organizational problems and processes. The organization begins a number of initial projects that focus on major priorities in production, service, and culture. During this phase, both consultants help to:

- Implement initial projects.
- Expand the TQM infrastructure.
- Build teams.
- Align process and policy management with the organization's mission, values, and principles.
- Transform the culture.
- Expand the overall effort.

These activities follow this approximate order, although some may begin simultaneously. With the exception of the initial projects, they are all ongoing activities that require a great deal of simultaneous effort. All these activities must happen for the implementation phase to be complete.

Implement Initial Projects

The OD and PI consultants work together with the organization to identify initial projects. The OD consultant's primary concern is selecting efforts that address cultural problems, and the PI consultant helps select projects that address major production and service outputs. Support for those efforts must be carefully planned and agreed upon by both consultants and senior management, and an interim diagnosis must also be planned.

The nature of the initial projects largely depends on the overall climate in the organization. At one point, we began work with two small printing companies that were almost exactly opposite in terms of culture. One had a very open and participative culture, while the other was more typically closed and autocratic. At the former, the initial projects addressed primarily technical issues concerned with waste, rework, and spoilage. Since employee-management relations seemed very good, there was less immediate need to address social issues. At the second company, both the OD and PI consultants felt that the initial projects should address cultural issues, because of the low morale and lack of trust between management and employees. Before getting to technical projects, it was important to demonstrate that management cared about the employees and that this would benefit them all, not just the stockholders. Without this kind of trust and morale, it is an uphill battle to find people who will go out of their way to improve the organization.

Expand the TQM Infrastructure

With the beginning of actual process improvement projects, the initial structure that was established to lead the effort must now be expanded. The OD consultant helps senior management understand the need for additional structures, such as Local Steering Committees and Quality Leadership Teams, and identify the procedures for putting them in place. This expansion provides more line authority and creates the support structure for process improvement and cultural change.

The first Local Steering Committees are established with the line management that is closest to the actual processes the organization needs to address. There is seldom a recipe for the structure or number of Local Steering Committees. The Executive Steering Committee and the consultants should work out a structure that is adequate for the processes that have been identified, the resources that can be allocated, and the goals to be accomplished.

Quality Leadership Teams may need to be established to address ongoing social issues, and other structures may be needed for establishing relationships with suppliers and partnerships with customers, labor-management participation, increased employee involvement, training and education, and other specific issues for which responsibility and accountability should be assigned to a group, function, team, or individual.

It is important not to create a bureaucracy during this expansion of the TQM effort. This can be avoided if the consultants make sure that management clearly understands the issues and priorities. Any structures must have clear goals and accountability and be part of the organization's priorities in terms of rewards, recognition, measurement criteria, and time frames.

For instance, at a large healthcare organization, the Executive Steering Committee first worked out its overall plan and charter. It then decided to establish similar leadership teams at each hospital and other healthcare provider sites. This meant addressing the need for more union involvement, education, and support for each site. An effort that started with senior management and union leadership was now ready to be expanded throughout the entire organization.

Build Teams

The entire TQM effort requires teamwork, both in leading the effort and in actual process improvement. On a short-term basis, the OD consultant oversees the need for teambuilding skills so that all committees, task forces, and teams have the skills to be effective. Over the long term, the OD consultant works to develop and train a core of facilitators.

Align Process and Policy Management with the Organization's Mission

In the early stages of TQM, it is important to focus on developing a corporate mission statement that is strategically aligned with the goals of total quality. TQM introduces a number of assumptions that challenge traditional business management and organization. The OD consultant initiates the first steps by having senior management test the organization's mission and values against the principles and values implicit in TQM.

At a company that made wire and cable products in California, the OD consultant and senior management spent one day identifying the company's primary vision, mission, and values. We then created a matrix placing the organization's goals and values down the side and Deming's Fourteen Points across the top. Discussing the relationships between the organization's stated values and those of Deming led to an expanded company vision for management. Conversely, they made some very good points that Deming does not address, such as the need to be concerned with the environment.

The next step for the organization is to integrate its mission and values with the process management activities that are already underway. Business planning and TQM planning are often regarded as two separate activities. As managers develop a greater understanding of TQM, they begin to realize that basic planning—financial, strategic, marketing, and so on—need to be integrated with the overall quality strategy. One method for integrating these activities is policy management (Mizuno 1988), which is a means of aligning organizational goals and objectives both vertically and horizontally. This ensures that priorities are set with a clear focus on the organization's mission and major objectives, and it sets the stage for further process improvement efforts throughout the organization. The OD consultant works with senior management to start this effort and monitor progress.

Timing is critical for policy management. If it is introduced too late, the organization will probably have worked on projects and tasks of low priority. If it is introduced too early, it will fail because most managers will not be able to distinguish it from traditional management by objectives (MBO). In MBO systems, goals and objectives are often established with no understanding of the true capability of the process. This often leads to suboptimization of the system, in which certain operations and functions achieve their goals and targets but at an overall loss to the organization.

Purchasing decisions based on lowest cost are one example of suboptimization. Thus, a purchasing manager following standard operating procedures might be viewed as doing a good job, even though the negative effects on the overall system far outweigh the advantage of lowest cost. At Pearl Harbor Naval Shipyard, many employees noted that the materials being purchased were a major source of rework and quality problems, and that it might be cheaper in the long run to purchase higher-quality materials even though the initial cost is greater. Without looking at the impact of short-term goals and quotas on an entire process, suboptimization is almost certain to occur. It generally takes several years for managers to learn how to establish process capability and to start using the tools in daily operations.

Transform the Culture

Management is typically concerned with costs, quantities, and schedules, while labor is concerned with wages, benefits, and working conditions. If carried to an extreme, these differing priorities can lead to labor strife, grievances, strikes, absenteeism, high turnover, and low morale. A fundamental tenet of TQM is that management must be just as concerned about wages, benefits, and working conditions as employees are. Since management controls these conditions, it is management's responsibility to see that continuous improvement efforts are made in these areas.

The major goal is to establish one or more Quality Leadership Teams to address problems with culture, quality of worklife, leadership, communication, and morale. The forms that these groups take depend on the organization's size, structure, and union involvement, but they usually consist of managers from a cross-section of the organization. At Blandin Paper Company, an effort to address these issues had been underway for several years through an active employee involvement group. If such efforts have been successful, the consultants will leave well enough alone.

One of the OD consultant's biggest challenges is to educate management about changing some of the assumptions that underlie traditional practices. This can bring the consultant into direct opposition to the organization's accepted ways of doing business. The OD consultant works with senior management as a team and with individual managers one-on-one to find mutually agreeable solutions to these problems. In a union environment, the OD consultant must also see that union leadership is included in all planning for the TQM process, and joint union-management committees may address these issues.

At one government establishment, the union had filed a grievance against an earlier quality circle program. The grievance was upheld by a court judge who ruled that all such activities had to cease until an agreement was reached with the union concerning procedures. The consultants spent considerable time on developing trust and a good working relationship that would bring the unions and management together on TQM implementation. Unfortunately, many organizations see TQM as a management program and do not understand the importance of the union's role in this effort.

Expand the Overall Effort

The initial projects mark the beginning of the implementation phase. When the organization is comfortable that it can successfully manage these projects, it must begin to plan for expanding the overall effort. Much of this work is tied into the process and policy management plans already underway. The OD consultant's expertise in systems, human resource development, and planning, ensures that expansion plans are well thought out and that they address both social and technical issues.

The Continuous Improvement Phase

The continuous improvement phase marks the beginning of the organization's self-development in TQM. At this point, much of the basic education and training has been accomplished. The structures for continuous improvement efforts have been developed. The mission, values, principles, and critical objectives have been defined. The initial projects have been completed and reviewed to see what was done well and what could have been done better. Ongoing efforts are in place to address cultural issues. In-house experts have been trained and developed to take over the roles of both the OD and PI consultants.

Although the organization has already accomplished a great deal, in many ways TQM does not really begin until this stage. Of course, unless all of the foregoing has been accomplished, no organization is ready for continuous improvement.

The most important issues for the OD consultant are to:

- Integrate the mission, values, and objectives with company-wide continuous improvement activities.
- Review internal and external customer needs/expectations.
- Review supplier relationships.
- Design cross-functional management.
- Ensure ongoing audits and diagnoses.
- Develop rewards, feedback, and recognition systems.

Integrate the Mission, Values, and Objectives with Company-Wide Continuous Improvement Activities

The company begins to roll out system-wide efforts at continuous improvement. The consultant's role is to see that the organization does not take any shortcuts and fall back into old patterns of communicating and directing. As barriers arise, the OD consultant works with senior and line management to understand the reasons for problems and delays, and emphasizes the need to understand what did *not* work as well as what did. One can learn as much from failure as from success.

Review Internal and External Customer Needs/Expectations

The primacy of the customer is one of the most fundamental concepts in TQM. In the early stages, the OD and PI consultants worked to build a focus on the customer as the target for all activities, and to educate people about the tools and methods that will help them understand the needs of both internal and external customers. As

TQM proceeds, even greater efforts are needed to track the key customer measures that are being established and to monitor the ability of the system to meet these needs. The OD consultant works with management and management information systems to establish such an information system that will provide the data for monitoring and evaluating the TQM effort.

Review Supplier Relationships

An organization's relationship with its suppliers directly affects its overall efficiency and effectiveness. The OD consultant works with the client to establish a strategy for continuously improving these relationships. This is a highly cooperative strategy based on the concepts of win–win bargaining.

Win–win bargaining has been described as a means of finding solutions where everyone gains and no one loses. It is a strategy that looks for common goals among the participants and lets them work together to meet those goals. Inco-Manitoba, for example, has established supplier partnerships based on long-term contracts that provide maximum benefit to both parties: Inco receives materials at lower cost, while the supplier is better able to plan for the future and make major investment decisions that might otherwise be deemed too risky.

Design Cross-Functional Management

At some point it is necessary to coordinate a number of activities and processes that cut across all units in the organization. Suboptimization can occur horizontally as well as vertically in an organization unless there is a mechanism to coordinate priorities and allocation of resources across departments and functions. The OD consultant works with management to design this mechanism. Typically, the first steps of policy management are seen as a method of vertical integration, while the later steps focus on cross-functional management for horizontal integration of priorities and resources.

Ensure Ongoing Audits and Diagnoses

The PDCA Cycle calls for regular checks and diagnoses as part of any process improvement activity. Without checking, it is difficult if not impossible to understand what worked and what did not. Furthermore, without checking the target (customer needs and expectations), continuous improvement is impossible. Both the OD and PI consultants help design a system of internal audits and diagnoses for systematic and ongoing checks. The OD consultant's background in survey techniques and human resource management ensures that these checks do not become forms of inspection or methods of assigning blame. Both consultants model the effort by conducting regular checks on the overall TQM effort and the client's satisfaction with the consultants.

It is possible to go overboard with diagnoses and audits, particularly if they occur before employees trust the aims and intentions of management. According to memos from the CEO at Florida Power & Light, a very prominent TQM organization that won the Deming Prize, the company had created a "quality bureaucracy." Steps were taken to dismantle this bureaucracy, one of which was to suspend the quality audit and diagnosis procedures that had been part of the TQM effort. (Many employees interpreted this as a retreat from quality and a return to the old way of doing business.)

Develop Rewards, Feedback, and Recognition Systems

Some of the most difficult issues in TQM concern the role of performance appraisals, financial rewards, employee recognition systems, promotion, and disciplinary policy. These issues are complicated by government policies, competitive pressures, and societal expectations.

Many existing policies and practices need to be improved as part of ongoing cultural improvement. The OD consultant is less likely to have existing prejudices and patterns that can keep the organization from taking a creative approach to these issues. However, the OD consultant's role is not to tell the organization what to do, but to help it develop its own resources for addressing these areas on a continuing basis.

In almost every organization there are painfully visible symbols of the status and privileges that divide management from employees. These may be minor things such as ties, parking privileges, offices, and cafeterias, but often they are very damaging to morale. We have seen situations such as inspections of employees before leaving facilities but not of management, grossly differential treatment for male and female employees, and sick-leave and time-off polices that were not based on any fair or equitable procedure.

THE PROCESS IMPROVEMENT (PI) CONSULTANT

Role and Objectives

The role of the PI consultant is not to tell others how to manage, but to demonstrate how statistical thinking improves everyday planning and decision making, to provide expertise in statistical theory and application, and to work hand in hand with employees as they apply these new methods.

The PI and OD consultants use different methods to help transform an organization. The PI consultant primarily coaches teams and individuals in applying a disciplined approach to improving work processes. The OD consultant focuses more on helping the senior management identify and overcome organizational barriers to improvement. There is a fair amount of overlap, since PI teams run into barriers such as managers who are threatened by a perceived loss of power, employees who are unsure about how this new work will affect their performance reviews, or existing standards that reward short-term gains over long-term improvement.

Both consultants are in positions that allow them to raise these issues and help the organization overcome them, but they must avoid the trap of trying to solve clients' problems for them. Instead, the consultant must transfer the necessary skills so that clients can better understand processes, identify causes of problems, and implement well-founded solutions themselves.

The Need for Statistical Thinking

Statistical thinking and methodology plays an integral role in the TQM transformation. As Walter Shewhart stated, "the long-range contribution of statistics depends not so much upon getting a lot of highly trained statisticians into industry as it does on creating a statistically minded generation of physicists, chemists, engineers, and others who will in any way have a hand in developing and directing the production processes of tomorrow" (Shewhart 1939, p.49).

Clearly, the need for statistical thinking is great in business, industry, and government. Unfortunately, much of the current workforce is illiterate in basic statistical concepts. Many people have a distaste for statistics brought on by courses that spent too much time memorizing formulas and not enough time discussing the overall concepts, benefits, and cultural issues in applying the methods. This has created a serious lack of knowledge at all levels—managers, supervisors, and workers.

Statistics is an easily abused science. Even the most basic concepts are commonly misunderstood, and mass training by too many unqualified individuals fosters misapplication. Care must be taken to learn from a qualified statistical or PI consultant who is well versed in both theory and application. Most people, however, don't know when to ask for help from a statistician. If they do ask, it is generally too late. This situation is aggravated by the myth that statistics is something you do to data once it has been collected. Unfortunately, no amount of good statistics can make up for bad data. To be useful, statisticians must be involved throughout the planning stage, not just during analysis.

Statistical methodology is not a separate element of the transformation; it has an impact on everything, including awareness of customer needs, management decisions, monitoring change and improvement, and employee involvement.

Focus on the Customer

Focusing on the customer involves creating operational definitions of customer requirements, understanding the relationship between measures of customer requirements and measures of process performance, and a methodology for continually monitoring and improving process performance. Key questions for managers are:

- What are the customers' current needs? Do the products and services currently meet those needs?
- What are the customers' future needs? What processes will meet these future needs?

Management Leadership

Leadership of the TQM effort requires decision making based on data, recognizing the interaction between processes and people, and developing processes to manage the quality of products and services.

- How can the level of quality be measured?
- What monitors are needed to assess whether quality is improving?

- What type of actions does the data indicate should be taken?
- What organizational barriers hinder improvement efforts? How can they be overcome?

Constant Improvement and Innovation

Continuous improvement and innovation require identifying sources of variation, a methodology to test possible cause-and-effect relationships, and monitoring the effect of changes to the process.

- Are the processes capable of meeting customer needs?
- What is most in need of improvement?
- How should resources be allocated to the various opportunities for improvement and innovation?
- How much rework is automatically built into the process?
- Do improvements have a lasting effect?
- Where should experimental designs be utilized?
- What are the organization's strengths and weaknesses relative to its competition?

Total Employee Involvement

Employee involvement calls on statistics as a common language, and uses data as a means to empower teams and individuals and as an aid in consensus decision making.

- What training in process improvement tools and techniques is needed?
- How can employees be empowered to make decisions?
- Do standard operating procedures reflect the best current methods? Are they consistently followed?
- What keeps employees from taking pride in their work, and how can this be eliminated?
- What are the employees' concerns about quality of worklife?

Key Concepts

The PI consultant helps clients discover how statistical thinking and methodology can improve the decision-making process. There are several key statistical concepts involved in this discovery:

- All work is a process.
- Quality must be defined in terms of customer requirements.
- Suboptimization of a process occurs whenever customers and suppliers are omitted from the improvement efforts.
- Variation is inherent in the output of any process.
- Improvement requires understanding the nature and sources of variation and then eliminating them one by one.
- Not understanding variation leads to inappropriate actions (tampering and making things worse).
- Possible cause-and-effect relationships should be validated before large-scale implementation of possible solutions.

These key concepts must first be understood by management. The consultant helps turn these concepts into methods that can be incorporated into daily work.

Working with the Executive Steering Committee

The role of the Executive Steering Committee is to lead the transformation. While the OD consultant helps the Committee create an environment for improvement and change, the PI consultant helps the Committee incorporate statistical thinking into the business planning process, learning the distinction between special and common causes, the effects of tampering, and practices that lead to suboptimized processes. Both consultants use formal training courses as well as one-on-one coaching.

The PI consultant works with the Executive Steering Committee to:

- Plan the transformation and monitor progress.
- Understand and apply process improvement tools and techniques.
- Establish measures of quality.
- Identify and resolve cross-functional issues.

Plan the Transformation and Monitor Progress

Planning the transformation involves clarifying both the client's and the consultants' expectations, establishing a working relationship, setting objectives, determining the pace, and allocating resources. The OD consultant estimates the time that the Executive Committee needs to devote to leading the effort, and the PI consultant estimates the time teams need to begin generating successes. Widespread implementation requires resources for the targeted areas for initial and latter improvement efforts and ongoing training. Starting more teams than management can support, or training more people than can be utilized, only leads to frustration and cynicism. Often there is a feeling that time spent planning merely delays the real work of improvement. During this time, however, the consultants begin to teach management about the nature of improvement and the potential barriers to progress. This allows management to prevent problems instead of merely reacting to them.

One aspect of the planning process is to identify initial project areas. In one healthcare organization, the PI consultant first interviewed each member of the Steering Committee to uncover problems for initial projects. The lengthy list of problems was narrowed down and resulted in nine project teams that the Steering Committee felt capable of supporting. In another healthcare organization, the Steering Committee went through a similar process and determined they were capable of supporting only three teams.

The result of the planning phase is a road map jointly developed and agreed to by the client and the consultants. This road map outlines the specific activities for various individuals and teams, as well as the role that both the OD and PI consultants will play with each one. The Executive Committee must ensure that all parties understand and carry out the road map. The PI consultant helps the Committee define realistic measures of progress and ensures appropriate analysis and follow-up. These measures might include the number of documented case studies, the number of individuals trained, the amount of time the Committee spends applying the tools to improve processes, or the number of processes that have been improved. These measures are needed for periodically checking and adjusting the plan. Without these checks, the transformation will be hindered by unforeseen problems.

Understand and Apply Process Improvement Tools and Techniques

No amount of formal instruction allows one to master process improvement tools and techniques. The best way for the Executive

Committee to learn is to apply the concepts to its own work under the PI consultant's guidance.

The concept of process is often difficult for managers to understand because they don't see the repetitive nature of much of their work. (Given the amount of time they spend fighting fires, it's easy to see why.) The PI consultant can help a manager select and flowchart an appropriate process to improve, such as creating a yearly budget, equipment purchase decisions, communicating the strategic plan, or creating a report. Since managers are frequently removed from the work processes, they tend to omit key steps and decision points. Hence, it is necessary to review and refine the process definition until it reflects the consensus of the team. At this point, the manager usually begins to see how little consistency there is in the way the work is done and how much time is spent correcting errors. The consultant helps the manager apply statistical methods to observe the process, uncover problems, and identify and validate possible causes.

Establish Measures of Quality

Most organizations use a set of management figures to run daily operations and plan for the future. These tend to be accounting figures, such as costs, quantity, revenue, and overtime. Quality may be reflected in figures for scrap, rework, warrantee, and customer complaints, but all too often nothing is done with this data. The PI consultant works with the Executive Committee to determine the most important figures needed to run the business and to develop appropriate methods of analysis. The consultant raises many questions: Does the data indicate how well the products and services meet customer requirements? Which processes influence the data? Does the method of analysis let one distinguish between special and common causes? Is there agreement about what the data means? What actions need to be taken?

Existing management figures provide a useful starting point to address these questions, uncover gaps in the information, and lead to the creation of appropriate quality measures. In a company that processes woodchips into various products, the PI consultant used management's daily reports to summarize key figures such as equipment downtime, product quality, and production volume. Appropriate analysis using control charts helped the Committee identify a shift in the process that had resulted in lower product quality.

Identify and Resolve Cross-Functional Issues

Few organizations have well-defined methods to deal with cross-functional issues. The Executive Committee is by nature a cross-functional team and must address these problems. The consultant uncovers functional barriers that impede PI Teams and decrease the effectiveness of PI Advisors. Teams themselves frequently lack the power or authority to cross these functional boundaries. Likewise, a Local Steering Committee may be able to influence only its own department. Both the OD and PI consultants work with the Committee to clarify priorities and coordinate efforts. Otherwise, as improvement efforts multiply, teams may feel they are competing for resources or that their goals are at odds with another team's. This competitive environment ultimately leads to suboptimization.

Working with the Local Steering Committee

The role of the Local Steering Committee is to carry out the planned transformation and thereby integrate TQM philosophy and methodology into everyday work. Both the PI and OD consultants work with the Local Committee to:

- Establish process management.
- Plan ongoing education and training.
- Manage communications.
- Lead by example.

Establish Process Management

The PI consultant helps to ensure that the Local Steering Committee consists of the right members, and that they understand their roles and responsibilities within the organization. Both consultants are often called on to describe specific activities that the Local Committee will be involved in and how much time they will need to dedicate to the effort. The PI consultant must also understand the existing culture in order to help the Committee create a plan that addresses their specific concerns and needs.

The pace of the Committee's activities depends on the size of the organization. Committee members in smaller organizations may be only one or two levels from the work processes, and will move more quickly to implementation. In very small organizations, the Executive and Local Steering Committees will be one and the same. In larger organizations, the pace must be slower in order to involve all levels of management. The consultant needs to work with both the Local Committee and middle management to ensure quality management concepts are present throughout the organization.

Process management first requires a thorough understanding of process improvement methods. Just as for the Executive Committee, the best way for the Local Committee to learn is for its members to work on improving their own processes under the guidance of the consultant. This gives them a working knowledge of the process, tools, techniques, and incremental nature of improvement. These initial projects also give them the opportunity to demonstrate their commitment to TQM.

Process management begins with identifying key processes, quality measures, and customer requirements. Simple brainstorming usually reveals the Committee's inability to distinguish processes from goals and objectives, and the PI consultant can challenge the members' understanding at this point.

Once consensus is reached on the processes they own, the Local Committee must determine appropriate measures of quality. While this may seem straightforward, it is usually a difficult task, because measures of quality may be neither obvious nor readily available. The PI consultant guides the initial definition, collection, and interpretation of this data. It takes a few trial efforts to define some useful measures and avoid mountains of useless data.

Finally, the PI consultant challenges the current understanding of customer requirements. Statistically sound survey and interviewing techniques are invaluable tools for obtaining well-founded customer information. This leads to operationally defined customer requirements that provide measurable indicators of how well processes are doing what they are supposed to do.

Process management is a method to prioritize improvement activities. Some of these priorities require commissioning PI Teams to address specific problems. The PI consultant works to ensure their success by helping the Local Committee assemble the right team members, provide training and resources, and establish methods of communication. In a large academic organization, for example, a process that involved three departments was selected for improvement. When the team was first assembled, it was discovered that one department had selected only high-level managers, even though the consultant's guidelines clearly stated that team members needed to be close to the day-to-day work. After further discussions with the Steering Committee, and before the team starting working, the membership was changed.

Plan Ongoing Education and Training

In the rush to get started, training often begins without considering the needs of the organization. The PI and OD consultants work together to assess training needs. The PI consultant identifies skills needed in basic process improvement tools and techniques, survey design, quality management concepts, and advanced statistical methods such as experimental design and reliability. The consultant matches the level of training with the individual's job requirements.

The consultant addresses participant selection, course customization, instructor certification, delivery methods, and applications follow-up and support. A plan can then be created for more effective training and resource utilization. Methods to assess the effectiveness of training and education must also be established to help plan for the continuing education and training of employees. In a large financial company, the PI consultant walked through the standard course material with the internal trainers. This allowed the consultant to check the trainers' understanding of content and their ability to relate concepts to specific company examples. A company case study was also developed to give the participants experience applying the tools and techniques to a process similar to their own.

Manage Communications

The Local Committee must establish a format for regular reviews with PI Teams. The consultant ensures that these reviews support the needs of the team and do not merely focus on results. These reviews should describe not only what the team has accomplished, but also the methods they used to reach their recommendations. Frustration occurs when managers try to force their own solutions rather than understand how the PI Teams arrived at their recommendations. The consultant models the kinds of questions the Committee should ask teams in order to identify barriers to progress, ensure adequate support, and demonstrate commitment to their efforts.

Improvement efforts and achievements need to be recognized,

yet the Local Committee may be looking for large-scale improvements and not notice small, incremental ones. The PI consultant must call attention to the small wins.

Lead by Example

Quality is often something that Local Committee members focus on only during official TQM meetings or when a consultant is present. The PI consultant helps the Committee improve its own team process and foster the use of statistical methods, a standard improvement process, and involving the people closest to the work. A manager who commissions a team to improve a process, but who tampers and refuses to involve others, does not fully understand TQM. A consultant needs to observe managers during their daily work, obtain feedback from subordinates, and then work to resolve these concerns with each individual manager. One person's traditional management behavior can destroy the efforts of many to change the culture.

Working with Process Improvement Advisors

PI Advisors provide internal expertise in process improvement tools and techniques. The consultant first works with management to clarify the roles of the PI Advisors, select candidates, gain the support of their immediate supervisors, plan their initial training, and position them in the organization to best utilize their strengths. The consultant then works closely with each PI Advisor to develop the skills for three roles:

1. Applications Consultant
2. Internal Consultant
3. Process Improvement Methods Instructor

Applications and Internal Consultants

The consultant's goal is to transfer skills so that PI Advisors can eventually assume their own consulting roles. The Advisors must learn not only how to work with teams, but how to seek out problems that no one else would uncover. This leads to establishing their role on the Local Steering Committee as a resource to identify opportunities for and barriers to improvement.

The consultant is a mentor for Advisors as they learn to facilitate PI Teams. The consultant first demonstrates how to establish one's role as a facilitator and advisor with the team leader and members. The consultant then shows how to keep teams focused on their mission, check ground rules, follow the improvement process, and plan the next step. Specific advice on how to apply process improvement tools, document progress, and present recommendations to the Local Committee also needs to be given.

In one organization, the PI consultant led the initial teams through one and a half days of start-up activities. This helped the teams solidify their mission and create an initial action plan. After these first meetings, the team leader and facilitator worked with the team through the problem-solving process. Every six weeks, the PI consultant, team leader, and facilitator would meet to discuss progress to date, answer specific questions, and guide future plans.

The first experience in application should be the PI Advisor's own work, which provides a safe environment for applying the concepts and getting feedback from the consultant. Next, the Advisor should observe the consultant facilitate a PI Team, followed by a discussion about specific applications and the team process. Finally, the consultant should observe the Advisor facilitate a team and provide constructive feedback about avoiding common pitfalls, such as accepting responsibility for solving the team's problems or taking on all the undesirable tasks.

The consultant works to establish a network among the Advisors so they might better learn from each other. Roundtable discussions, for example, provide opportunities to present case studies, discuss their difficulties, frustrations, and successes, and develop a support system. The consultant can also use such a forum to provide continuing education in advanced statistical methods and in facilitating, consulting, and instructional skills.

Process Improvement Methods (PIM) Instructor

The consultant first ensures that each PI Advisor understands the theory and has had success in its application. While all Advisors will be Applications Consultants, not all will become PIM Instructors. The consultant helps the Executive Steering Committee develop a process for selecting and training PIM Instructors. For example, the consultant may recommend a train-the-trainer course for those lacking instructor skills. Customizing the training materials is often a step in the instructional process, and the consultant helps the Advisors develop sound, logical, and relevant examples and case studies. Team teaching with the PI consultant provides an opportunity for them to enhance both their process improvement and instructional skills.

A group of internal trainers in one organization held practice teaching sessions with the PI consultant. This provided them a safe environment to check their understanding of content and knowledge of instructional methods. The participants were able to learn from the consultant as well as from themselves.

Working with Process Improvement Teams

PI Teams typically focus on a single process or problem. These teams meet regularly, usually weekly or biweekly, and disband when a desired level of improvement is achieved. The PI consultant does not usually facilitate numerous teams for various reasons: teams meet more frequently than the consultant is available, the consultant should not assume the role of the PI Advisor, and teams are better served by facilitators who are familiar with the organization. However, the consultant does need to be involved with teams when:

- PI Advisors are not be available for pilot projects.
- The Local Steering Committee does not understand how to select projects.
- The Executive Steering Committee does not understand what it means to empower teams or how to do it.
- The Executive Steering Committee does not know how to assess team progress.

In each of these cases, the PI consultant provides the knowledge and hands-on support until internal resources can assume these roles.

WHEN THE CONSULTANT'S ROLE IS OVER

The consultant's goal is to help create an environment where statistical thinking and methods are used in everyday decision making and long-range business planning. This can only be done through a partnership with the client. The pace of the transformation must be one the organization can support over the long term, the style must fit the organizational culture, and recognition must be given to all who participate. A consultant's success is determined not only by what the client is currently able to achieve, but by whether the client's future success outlives the consultant's active involvement.

The PI consultant will have transferred to the internal PI advisors much of the knowledge and skills to be able to make more confident decisions. In some cases, the organization may decide to hire a permanent employee to work in the statistical area or to send a PI Advisor to school for more training and to become a company statistician.

The OD consultant will have worked very closely with both the training department and the TQM Coordinator to help ensure that a number of people can continue the work that was started. Much of the work that the OD consultant was coordinating will be taken over by the TQM Coordinator, who at some point will feel confident about the goals and objectives of TQM. Since the work of the OD consultant touches many areas, many of the consultant's responsibilities will have been assigned to specific managers, labor teams, employee involvement teams, or management teams. These individuals and groups will be accountable for continuing to work to change the organizational culture.

Both consultants should have helped the organization acquire the skills and knowledge to continue the transformation on its own. There is no definite schedule for ending the client-consultant relationship, since this depends on client readiness and the perceived value of the consultant's contributions. Nevertheless, there comes a time when one or both consultants will see that the organization is capable of working on its own.

Generally, it is best to avoid an abrupt ending to a client–consultant relationship, and we usually try to phase out work by going to a less frequent schedule. If we were meeting with the client monthly, for example, we might phase out by meeting every other month, then quarterly, and then scheduling a final visit involving an assessment or audit and a final report. We also conduct an annual survey of our clients and all those with whom our relationship is ending. This provides us with data concerning their feelings about our role with them during the TQM effort. The knowledge gained from these surveys and final assessments is helpful in the continual improvement of the transformation model.

9

The Union and Management

ROBERT KILLEEN

*United Auto Workers (retired) and the Minnesota Council for
Quality*

The union is a vital element in many organizations. Because TQM
promotes employee involvement and quality-of-worklife programs,
labor-management cooperation is essential when these areas are affected by the transformation.

The major responsibilities of union and management leadership
in the TQM transformation are to:

- Establish the key players and responsibilities.
- Establish a means for involving all union leadership in train-
  ing, conferences, visits, consulting, and so on.
- Identify the major efforts that require the union's involvement.
- Ensure that union leadership will be able to participate as
  planned.

These overall responsibilities can be broken down into seven major
steps that both the union and management should follow (Persico,
Bednarczyk, and Negus 1989).

Management should:

1. Understand legitimate union concerns about changes in the
   work environment. Union leadership should not have to fer-
   ret out the implications of TQM.

2. Understand labor relations laws and how they affect union leadership and TQM implementation.

3. Give the union time to respond. Developing a consensus on TQM can be very time-consuming, as management should know.

4. Educate and treat the union as an equal partner in TQM. Sharing information with union leadership is necessary if there is to be a full, trusting partnership.

5. Define a legitimate, ongoing role for the union to help steer the TQM program. The union must not be given a minor or token role.

6. Work with the union on ways to handle TQM issues that overlap the collective bargaining agreement.

7. Define its position on job security. Some companies can promise no layoffs, but a TQM company relies on employees who feel secure.

The union should:

1. Understand TQM philosophy and methods so it can provide true leadership in the transformation.

2. Form its own steering committee to represent its membership in TQM decision making.

3. Define a role for all union leaders, and provide them with training to understand TQM and work cooperatively with management.

4. Keep union membership regularly informed about TQM issues, goals, activities, and achievements.

5. Work with management on job security issues. Job security is critical to the success of TQM, but recognize that management's commitment to job security depends on the overall strength of the company.

6. Work with management on ways to handle TQM issues that overlap the collective bargaining agreement.

7. Establish a network with other unions involved in TQM. This can provide invaluable insight into TQM issues and problems.

This chapter, written by someone who has worked closely in labor relations on behalf of the unions, reflects on the need for a management-labor consensus in a successful TQM transformation.

THE FLAWED MANAGEMENT–LABOR RELATIONSHIP

Quality and productivity remain the most misunderstood terms in U.S. industrial and service organizations. Our falling market share is dramatic in many product segments, and a significant portion of the trade deficit is due to the ability of foreign competitors to deliver higher-quality products. When and how did U.S. manufacturers in virtually every major segment lose the capacity to compete and win?

After a forty-year career in industrial America—the greatest portion of it in the automobile industry—I have a sense of how we surrendered our edge. But a representative of our foreign competition has phrased the explanation most forcefully. Mr. Konosuke Matsushita, Executive Director of Matsushita Electric Industrial Company, Ltd., said:

> We [the Japanese] are going to win and the industrial West is going to lose out; there's not much you can do about it because the reasons for your failure are within yourselves. Your firms are built on the Taylor model. Even worse, so are your heads. With your bosses doing the thinking while the workers wield the screwdrivers, you're convinced deep down that this is the right way to run the business. (quoted in Tribus 1987)

This appraisal of our potential is shocking, partly because it so boldly challenges our American pride. But it also points out a flaw that can strangle even the most aggressive quality improvement program. This weak link is adversity and noncooperation between management and labor.

A TIME FOR EQUAL ACCOUNTABILITY

In spite of the recent rhetoric from both sides of the management-labor table, many organizations find that both camps have considerable ground to cover for TQM to succeed, mostly because suspicion and blame continue to override common sense. Both are typical of the American system. Unions blame management. Management blames unions and the workforce. Everything the United States needs to regain its competitive standing is contained in the principles of TQM. But the concept can move from theory to daily practice only if management provides for and invites full and equal participation by union leadership and its members.

When management makes the decision to start a TQM program, the union should automatically become a full partner in the effort. The solution to competitiveness, profitability, and job security is found only when groups look squarely at reality and diagnose what is wrong with processes and systems. Key direction and leadership by the union can be the element that leads to a true partnership and an environment where everyone wins.

A complete accounting of the union's objectives—the desired results—within TQM include:

- Greater job security
- Increased profitability
- Improved safety
- Lower absenteeism rates
- Increased respect for the company
- Increased respect for and confidence in the union
- Easier negotiations

If a union needs further justification to forego suspicion and provide the valuable information it possesses, it should consider TQM a long-awaited opportunity to have a voice and address the problems it has documented.

Don Rand, an administrative assistant during the middle 1970s to then UAW Secretary-Treasurer Emil Masey, tells a story about his visit with a group of employees at an automaker's piston ring plant. Rand had just told the workers that the plant was a disaster and would probably be closed unless it was fixed up. Some of the union members spoke up to place the blame on "stupid management that doesn't know how to run the plant and is doing everything wrong." Rand redirected the emotion of the moment to emphasize the real issue and the critical need for union involvement in a process like quality improvement. "You may be right," he told them. "But those stupid managers are going to lose you your jobs."

The new agenda for unions and their members—the first order of business every day—is to take the lead and do everything possible to implement TQM programs company-wide. The alternative is to continue slipping in the world marketplace. Winning the argument about who is to blame achieves absolutely nothing. It simply undercuts the labor force in the form of lost jobs, lower wages, and dwindling benefits. "Quality is our responsibility in the shop," two strong union leaders at the Harley-Davidson plant in Milwaukee told me. "When we see it slipping, we march into management's office and work with them to straighten it out. We are never going back to the days when damn near all of us lost our jobs because of poor quality."

This kind of relearning—taking a more productive perspective on relationships and cooperation—is an assignment for management as well. Many companies give lip service to TQM, rather than sincerely making the break with Taylorism and the past. The millions of dollars spent on union busting and bashing could pay real dividends in joining with unions and retraining workers to regain economic leadership.

Employers who ask me how they can reach their workers say, "They don't trust us." The extremes of noncommunication and nonparticipation became clear to me a couple of years ago when a consultant invited me to join him at dinner with the president of a large company, the production manager, and the industrial relations person. The evening was dominated by their inquiries about the union, its structure, and its members. But one question told me all I needed to know about the environment at the company. This same question has been asked of me on two other occasions: "How do I meet the local union president?"

TQM presents the perfect opportunity to correct this kind of operational malfunction. I believe unions will cooperate with TQM programs if they are informed and involved in the process from the very beginning. Union leaders and their members must be trusted to know the company's intentions and objectives. Beginning immediately, it will be very important for U.S. management–labor communication to be open, honest, and complete. Trust is built through the example of change.

TQM DOES WORK—EVEN IN EXTREME CONDITIONS

As evidence that a new management–labor partnership can be created and lead to success, I'd like to mention another dinner two years later with personnel from that same company. The occasion was a Deming seminar attended by the president, members of his support staff, the local union president, and one of his stewards. This time the conversation revolved around the company's success at increasing productivity to a level that no one would have believed possible under the previous system. The union had more members working than ever before, and they were participants in a new profitsharing plan.

One of the critical transformations in this particular example was a new face-to-face relationship between the company's top officer and union leadership. In a typical organization, there is likely to be some inconsistency in management receptiveness to greater union and worker involvement in company operations. Disparities along the management chain should be resolved at their respective sources. When this approach is unsuccessful, the only alternative is the involvement of top management. Unless executives at this level are committed to promoting a partnership with the union and are leading by example, the TQM program will not succeed.

A proactive approach by top executives to foster management consistency is to guarantee openly that union leaders will be members of the Executive Steering Committee and will be trained alongside company managers. It is also top management's responsibility to position the union as an equal partner in forming and operating individual TQM teams.

Expectations about implementing TQM should take into account the well-established attitudes, perceptions, and obstacles that must be neutralized or removed. Speed in establishing a new order in management-labor relations and TQM is in direct proportion to the layers of nonproductive corporate culture that must be stripped away.

One example of ingrained obstacles to productive management–labor relations is management's traditional reluctance to share information about out-sourcing or outside contracting in industrial plants. Most collective bargaining agreements limit management's ability to contract work outside the company because of costs, manpower constraints, available skills, and so on. The system has been in place for years, but very little of the information used by management in the decision-making process is considered credible by unions. Over the years, union suspicions about this particular impasse have resulted in hundreds of grievances.

At one plant, negotiations over this scenario prompted a union suggestion that would open the door to greater worker involvement: include a union representative on the company's make-buy committee. Management rejected the proposition but agreed to study it during the three-year term of the new agreement. At the halfway point of the contract, the company asked the union to select a member who would sit in on the committee's deliberations. The union representative added valuable information that helped the company retain work that otherwise would have been contracted outside. Perhaps more important, his presence also meant the union no longer had reason to question company data. The next contract included a provision for nonvoting union membership on the make-buy committee. As a result, there have been no out-sourcing grievances at that plant for the last two years.

There are many other management–labor improvements visible within those companies that have strived to replace Taylor-style autocracy with the principles of TQM. These include:

- Employee contact with vendors and customers
- Overlapping of hourly and salaried work
- Classification reductions
- Training programs developed by front-line workers
- Employee attendance at operational meetings
- Elimination of time clocks, privileged parking and dining rooms for executives
- Elimination of merit reviews
- Involvement in department and plant layout
- Union involvement in pension investment decisions
- Reductions in the amount of supervision required

There are two general caveats regarding TQM implementation. First, although union stewards throughout the company should be involved from the beginning of the TQM process, it can be counterproductive to establish a plant-wide program right away. TQM represents a significant change that can create far too many problems and barriers to handle on a plant-wide basis at first. Generally, it's better to implement the transformation department by department, starting with a small group that accepts and understands the quality objectives. As the success of that group becomes known, the program can be expanded. In plants that have used this start-up method, I have seen other sections demand that they be given a chance to try the new system.

Second, avoid trying to negotiate a TQM program into the collective bargaining agreement. Union contract negotiations are usually a complex, detailed, and exact "t-crossing and i-dotting" exercise concerning wages, hours, and working conditions. Expecting to negotiate a new TQM program into the contract is not realistic: few people understand what it is, and there is no set pattern for its implementation. It is more productive to discuss the subject and agree in principle to implement TQM during the term of the contract, and cover this agreement in a supplemental letter of understanding attached to the contract. This then gives you flexibility in implementing a TQM program during the contract period.

The nuts and bolts of a TQM program provide several opportunities to champion a new level of union involvement and worker empowerment. The union's role in the training that accompanies TQM is critical in this regard. Training should be an equal partnership aimed at turning more and more of its development and management over to departments and employees. Training messages refined by the workforce will be more effective and standards will be more demanding than is possible by using programs that are always developed and administered from the top down.

An example of this is seen at the FMC plant in Fridley, Minnesota, which has completely rebuilt its training programs in the last two three-year agreements (1986–92). All programs are now developed by joint committees of two or three supervisors, two or three hourly workers, and a union training coordinator. The training coordinator also watches for potential conflicts with the labor agreement. If the agreement needs to be modified, the recommended changes carry much greater credibility with the bargaining committee. Vic Hagenah, the union coordinator, and Don Bauer, the industrial relations manager, made these points:

- The progress review process is much more credible when employees are reviewed by their peers. It can be more honest than a supervisor's review, and is less likely to be challenged by the employee and the union.

- The development of training programs is more worker-directed. Training becomes much more related to the skills that are actually needed for improvement, and there is greater employee commitment to make the program work.
- Supervisors have an opportunity to transfer certain duties to employees, who indeed might be better at the work. This gives supervisors more time to lead their employees in teambuilding and quality improvement.

BUILDING A MANAGEMENT–LABOR CONSENSUS

In Minnesota, labor played a role in the development of an organization known as the Council for Quality, an outgrowth of a 1987 governor's commission to study the state's economic future. As chair of the commission's subcommittee on quality and productivity, I worked to build business and labor support for the bill that established the Council. I co-chaired the Council during its first two years and now continue as an advisor.

The mission of this nonpartisan, nonprofit coalition of state businesses is to make the phrase "Produced in Minnesota" synonymous with "Quality Second to None." The Council's broad-based educational and public awareness campaign is anchored by five basic points that were developed by our first executive-director, Dr. Walter Bruning, who was then on loan from Control Data Corporation. Borrowing from the best of the quality gurus, the points are a shortened version of what is needed to make TQM initiatives successful statewide. These points also suggest a common ground on which management–labor relationships of the future can be built.

- *Management leadership.* An effective quality effort demands commitment and involvement by the CEO and top management. Unless management's commitment is *visible* and credible, employees will not view the changes as important to the business. All employees have significant roles to play in quality improvement, but company leaders control eighty-five percent of the potential in this area. Lead your employees.
- *Employee participation.* Employee involvement and ownership of

TQM concepts are essential. Delegate responsibility. Empower employees by pushing decision making to the lowest possible level. Take advantage of employee knowledge and ideas for improvement. Train them in group problem-solving techniques. Reward innovation. Recognize employees for their contributions and ideas. Evaluate current management practices and eliminate barriers to positive behavior.

- *Sensitivity to customers.* Be sensitive to customers' needs and wants. Listen to customers and match products and processes to their current and future needs. Remember that customers are both internal and external to the organization. The person who receives your work is a customer, and customer satisfaction is your product.

- *Continuous improvement.* Develop the organization by focusing on the system as a whole. Promote group problem solving and identify barriers to teambuilding. Identify and continuously measure the improvement of all processes within the organization. Communicate with employees. Set standards for success. Recognize good performance. Harness creativity. Solicit suggestions. Use ergonomics. Make the job fit the person, not vice versa.

- *Employee training.* Champion education and training for all employees. Promote the functional use and understanding of the Seven Basic Tools of SPC, just-in-time methods, mission setting, teambuilding, long-range planning, decision-making techniques, communication, math, advanced technologies, and other integral skills specific to the future of the industry in which you compete.

EVERYONE WINS OR EVERYONE LOSES

A particular auto-related plant closed down in the mid-1980s. When the operation ceased and the jobs disappeared, the following statement was still part of the UAW agreement: "Employees shall not knowingly pass or process any defective work without authorization from the company."

The union had attempted several times over the years to have this language removed. It believed that the stipulation condoned, at least indirectly, poor quality products. During the same period, company management frequently had wrangled with labor over the cost of unemployment insurance and worker's compensation. In the end, there was nothing positive to show for all of the effort invested in mutual finger-pointing. The adversarial management–labor relationship left no room for either side to win.

TQM could have saved that plant. We know that it works. Foreign competitors who are committed to principles such as continuous improvement are advancing into new processes, systems, and manufacturing styles that are likely to maintain their quality advantage over America for at least the decade of the 1990s.

Management and labor in the United States can continue to face each other down and permit the accompanying erosion of business and jobs to become permanent. Or they can sit together on the same side of the table and use the proven policies and philosophies of TQM. America's economic destiny and quality of life are both within our control.

Appendix A

The Fourteen Points

The Fourteen Points formulated by Dr. Deming (see *Out of the Crisis*, 1986) serve as a starting point for the quality journey. Organizations need to translate these principles into their own terms, but the Fourteen Points are fundamental recommendations that management should not ignore.

1. Create constancy of purpose toward the improvement of product and service, with the aim to become competitive, stay in business, and provide jobs.
2. Adopt the new philosophy. We are in a new economic age. Western management must awaken to the challenge, learn its responsibilities, and take on leadership for change.
3. Cease dependence on inspection to achieve quality. Eliminate the need for mass inspection by building quality into the product in the first place.
4. End the practice of awarding business on the basis of price tag alone. Instead, minimize total cost. Move toward a single supplier for any one item, on a long-term relationship of loyalty and trust.
5. Improve constantly and forever the system of production and service, to improve quality and productivity, and thus constantly decrease costs.
6. Institute training on the job.
7. Institute leadership (see point 12). The aim of leadership should be to help people and machines and gadgets do a better job. Leadership of management is in need of overhaul, as well as leadership of production workers.

8. Drive out fear, so that everyone may work effectively for the organization.

9. Break down barriers between departments. People in research, design, sales, and production must work as a team, to foresee problems in producing and using the product or service.

10. Eliminate slogans, exhortations, and targets for the workforce asking for zero defects and new levels of productivity.

11. a. Eliminate work standards (quotas) on the factory floor. Substitute leadership.

    b. Eliminate management by objective. Eliminate management by numbers, numerical goals. Substitute leadership.

12. a. Remove barriers that rob hourly workers of their right to pride of workmanship. The responsibility of supervisors must be changed from sheer numbers to quality.

    b. Remove barriers that rob people in management and engineering of their right to pride of workmanship. This means, among other things, abolishment of the annual or merit rating and of management by objective, management by the numbers.

13. Institute a vigorous program of education and self-improvement.

14. Put everybody in the company to work to accomplish the transformation. The transformation is everybody's job.

Appendix B

The Seven Basic Tools

The Seven Basic Tools of SPC (Figure B.1) form the backbone of any quality improvement effort. They provide a way of putting data into a graphic format so that one can better understand work processes and systems, their capabilities, the variation within them, the probable causes of problems, and the priorities for improvement efforts. The tools are extremely useful in checking the effectiveness of countermeasures set into motion in the *Do* stage of the PDCA Cycle.

Cause-and-Effect Diagram. Cause-and-effect diagrams, also known as fishbone diagrams or Ishikawa diagrams, are helpful for generating and sorting ideas about the causes of variation within a process, and identifying the most likely causes of problems. These causes are grouped into categories, such as environment, materials, methods, equipment, and people.

Flowchart. A flowchart is a diagram that uses coded symbols, linear sequences, and yes/no decisions to define the steps in a process and to identify what a process does and what it should do. Integrated flowcharts also depict the participants in the process and their responsibilities.

Pareto Chart. Pareto charts, named after the Italian economist Vilfredo Pareto, are bar graphs that categorize the causes of a condition into the "vital few and the trivial many." Each bar represents one category, and its height represents the frequency of occurrence. The bars are arranged in descending order, from most to least important.

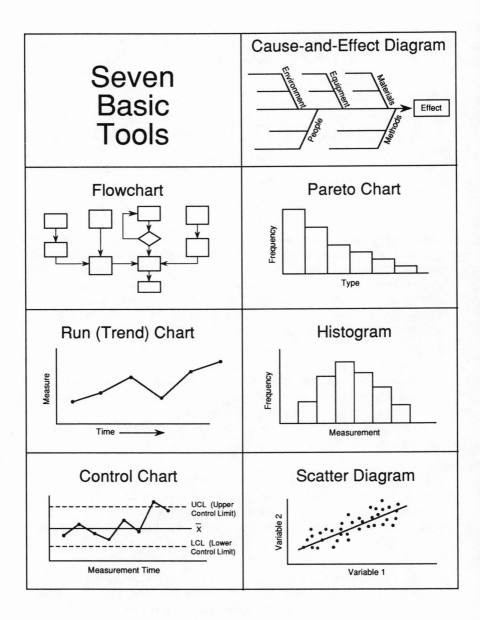

Seven Basic Tools

Cause-and-Effect Diagram

Environment Equipment Materials

People Methods

Effect

Flowchart

Pareto Chart

Frequency

Type

Run (Trend) Chart

Measure

Time

Histogram

Frequency

Measurement

Control Chart

UCL (Upper Control Limit)

$\bar{x}$

LCL (Lower Control Limit)

Measurement Time

Scatter Diagram

Variable 2

Variable 1

Run (Trend) Chart. Run charts show how a particular process characteristic varies over time. They are helpful for detecting trends, shifts, cycles, or other patterns.

Histogram. Histograms are bar graphs that show the frequency of variation in a single variable.

Control Chart. Control charts are used to detect special causes of variation that need to be eliminated from a process. Control charts show whether a process characteristic is stable and predictable, and can also help determine the capability of a process under the current system.

Scatter Diagram. Scatter diagrams are used to show whether there is any relationship between two variables. For example, a positive relationship is indicated if both variables increase, or a negative relationship if one variable increases as the other decreases.

Appendix C

The Seven New Management Tools

The Seven New Management Tools (Figure C.1) provide a graphic format for displaying verbal information about processes, systems, and causes of problems. They are particularly useful in the management planning process.

Affinity Diagram. Affinity diagrams are used to generate and categorize information about a process problem.

Interrelationship Diagraph. Interrelationship diagraphs use input from the affinity diagram to organize and identify the major cause-effect relationships among the various elements of a problem.

Systematic Diagram. Systematic diagrams, also known as tree diagrams or dendograms, show the relationships between problems and the actions that are needed to improve a process or product performance.

Matrix Diagram. Matrix diagrams are used to link organizational units with problems and to establish responsibility for improvement efforts.

Matrix Data Analysis (glyph). Matrix data analysis is a statistical technique to identify the strength of the relationships between process or product characteristics.

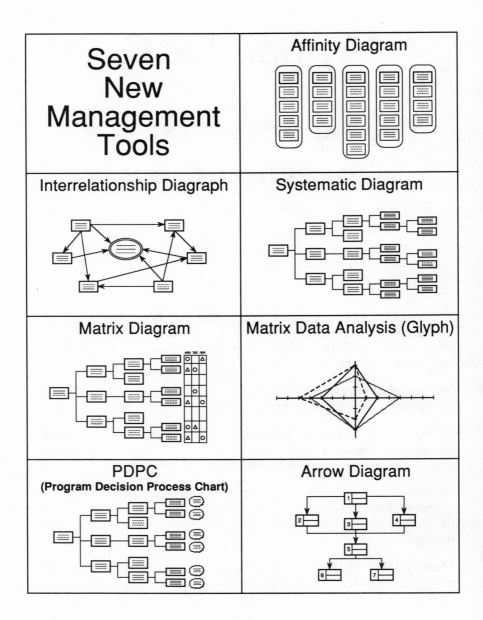

Seven New Management Tools

Affinity Diagram

Interrelationship Diagraph

Systematic Diagram

Matrix Diagram

Matrix Data Analysis (Glyph)

PDPC
(Program Decision Process Chart)

Arrow Diagram

Program Decision Process Chart (PDPC). Program decision process charts help determine which processes to use to obtain desired results by analyzing the sequence of events and the possible outcomes.

Arrow Diagram. Arrow diagrams are another name for PERT charts (Program Evaluation and Review Technique). These are used to plan a time sequence for managing a complex project or a process or product improvement effort when the steps can be determined in advance.

Glossary

Affinity diagram—One of the Seven New Management Tools. See Appendix B.

Applications Consultant—See: Process Improvement Advisor.

Arrow diagram—One of the Seven New Management Tools. See Appendix B.

ASQC—American Society for Quality Control, Milwaukee, Wisconsin.

Barriers—Problems or obstacles embedded in organizational policies and procedures that prevent the adoption of a quality culture.

Brainstorming—The purpose of brainstorming is to develop a hypothesis on root causes of a problem. Ideas are solicited from all team members concerning the perceived problem. Criticisms or judgments about the ideas being offered are not allowed during this process.

Capable process—A stable process that predictably meets customer requirements. This is a statistical state and not an opinion.

Cause-and-effect diagram—One of the Seven Basic Tools. Also called an Ishikawa or fishbone diagram. See Appendix A.

Champion—A member of the Executive Steering Committee who is accountable for leading the understanding and adoption of a particular Deming principle.

Common cause—A cause of variation that is inherent in the way the process is organized and operated.

Control chart—One of the Seven Basic Tools. See Appendix A.

Cost of ownership—The total cost to an organization to purchase and own products from a supplier. It is a function of price, dependability, percent defective, consistency, and any other relevant quality characteristic.

Critical mass—That number of persons in any organization who must be involved in the transformation in order to ensure self-sustaining progress.

Customer—The user of a product or service, either internal or external to the generating process. Within a system, the next process is considered the customer for a process.

Data collection—The process of gathering factual information regarding a process to be used as a basis for future decisions.

Executive Steering Committee—A committee composed of senior management from each of the major functional areas of the organization. The primary purpose is to plan, implement, check, and ensure that the necessary steps are being taken to develop a TQM organization. See also: Local Steering Committee.

Fishbone diagram (cause-and-effect diagram)—One of the Seven Basic Tools. See Appendix A.

Flowchart—One of the Seven Basic Tools. See Appendix A.

Glyph (matrix data analysis)—One of the Seven New Management Tools. See Appendix B.

GOAL/QPC—Growth Opportunity Alliance of Greater Lawrence, Springfield, Massachusetts.

Ground rules—The standards of behavior for PI Team meetings. These standards may cover attendance, communication, participation, decision making, and other issues that are important to the team. Ground rules interject discipline and structure into group dynamics.

Histogram—One of the Seven Basic Tools. See Appendix A.

Input—A resource introduced into a system or expended in its operation helping to attain a result or output.

Internal Consultant—See: Process Improvement Advisor.

Interrelationship diagraph—One of the Seven New Management Tools. See Appendix B.

Ishikawa diagram (cause-and-effect diagram)—One of the Seven Basic Tools. See Appendix A.

Local Steering Committee—A committee composed of a senior area manager (who is also on the Executive Steering Committee) and his or her immediate staff. The major purposes of the committee are to identify critical processes and customer requirements, develop quality measures, and implement a plan for continuous improvement under the guidance of the Executive Steering Committee. See also: Executive Steering Committee.

Malcolm Baldrige National Quality Award—Public Law 100–107, signed by President Ronald Reagan, establishes an annual United States National Quality Award. The purposes of the Award are to promote quality awareness, recognize quality achievements of U.S. companies, and publicize successful quality strategies.

Management by objectives (MBO)—A commonly used tool for appraising management performance. MBO assumes that performance can be measured best by comparing actual results with planned objectives.

Matrix data analysis (glyph)—One of the Seven New Management Tools. See Appendix B.

Matrix diagram—One of the Seven New Management Tools. See Appendix B.

MBO—See: Management by objectives.

Mission statement—A statement of aims and purposes for the organization.

OD—See: Organizational Development.

Optimization—The use of resources in as effective a way as possible under specified conditions.

Organizational Development (OD)—Organizational development relies on a consultant's expertise (primarily in the behavioral sciences) to improve the way an organization functions by focusing on how it approaches problem solving and decision making.

Output—The power, energy, or result produced by a system.

PACE—Philadelphia Area Council for Excellence.

Pareto chart—One of the Seven Basic Tools. See Appendix A.

PDCA Cycle—Plan–Do–Check–Act is a cycle that involves an interactive approach to process improvement and problem solving. Commonly referred to as the Shewhart Cycle, and also known as PDSA (Plan–Do–Study–Act).

PI—See: Process Improvement.

Policy management (deployment)—A management practice that aims to translate the organization's vision and goals into process- and team-oriented approaches throughout the workplace. It is a systematic process that begins with top management and cascades through the organization.

Process—A set of causes and conditions that repeatedly come together to transform inputs into outputs. A series of related tasks.

Process boundaries—Limits on the scope of actions taken to improve a process.

Process control—The act of achieving and maintaining a stable process.

Process improvement—A continual endeavor to learn about the cause-and-effect mechanisms in a process in order to reduce the complexity and variation brought about by common causes.

Process Improvement (PI) Advisor—Those organization members who act as an Applications Consultant, Process Improvement Methods (PIM) Instructor, or Internal Consultant.

Process Improvement Methods (PIM) Instructor—See: Process Improvement Advisor.

Process Improvement (PI) Team—The purpose of the PI Team is to work on any process or problem that is related to increasing customer satisfaction and/or is vital to the mission of the organization. PI teams consist of people who work in the process day to day, and the customers, suppliers, and supervisors of the process.

Process management—A methodology that views the organization as a system, determines which processes need improvement or control, sets priorities, and provides leadership to initiate and sustain process improvement efforts.

Profound knowledge—Knowledge a manager must possess to successfully transform an organization to the new philosophy. It consists of four interrelated parts: appreciation for a system, some knowledge of the theory of variation, a theory of knowledge, and an understanding of psychology.

Program decision process chart (PDPC)—One of the Seven New Management Tools. See Appendix B.

Purpose—The object or goal toward which one strives or for which something exists.

Quality improvement cycle—A process by which product quality can be heightened through improving the process that produced the product.

Quality journal—A seven-step structured procedure for studying processes with process improvement as the goal. The procedures are documented in a journal format.

Quality Leadership Team—Quality Leadership Teams represent a diagonal slice of the organization. Their objective is to identify and recommend to the Executive Steering Committee the removal of barriers to integrating the Fourteen Points. Also referred to as culture improvement teams.

Road map—A plan outlining the sequence of tasks that an organization will take to implement quality improvement.

Run (trend) chart—One of the Seven Basic Tools. See Appendix A.

Scatter diagram—One of the Seven Basic Tools. See Appendix A.

Seven Basic Tools—The Seven Basic Tools are cause-and-effect diagrams, flowcharts, Pareto charts, histograms, scatter diagrams, run charts, and control charts. See Appendix A for examples.

Seven New Management Tools—Tools that are useful for management in the planning process: affinity diagram, interrelationship diagraph, systematic diagram, matrix diagram, matrix data analysis (glyph), program decision process chart (PDPC), and arrow diagram. See Appendix B for examples.

Shewhart Cycle—See: PDCA Cycle.

SPC—See: Statistical process control.

Special cause—A cause of variation that is probably not always present or does not affect every part of the process, but that arises from special circumstances. Sometimes referred to as an assignable cause.

Stable process—A process that is subject to variation brought on only by common causes. The property of being in statistical control.

Statistical process control (SPC)—A method by which a process is studied through the use of statistics. The resulting data is used to make appropriate changes in the system to reduce variation in the output.

Steering Committee—See: Executive Steering Committee and Local Steering Committee.

Suboptimization—The failure to achieve optimum effectiveness from available resources in a given situation, especially by achieving optimum effectiveness for a subsystem but not the system as a whole.

Supplier—A person or organization, either internal or external, that provides goods or services for use by one or more customers.

System—A group of component items, tasks, or processes that are interdependent and may be identified and treated as an entity.

Systematic diagram—One of the Seven New Management Tools. See Appendix B.

Tampering—Adjusting a process that is in control and on target.

TQM—See: Total Quality Management.

Total Quality Management (TQM)—TQM is a management system that emphasizes process management, customer service, waste reduction, and people. *Total* means everyone participates, and that it is integrated into all business functions. *Quality* involves meeting or exceeding customer expectations. *Management* involves improving and maintaining business systems and their related processes.

Unstable process—A process that is subject to variation brought on by both common and special causes.

Variation—Quantitative change in value between cases or over time caused by common or special causes.

References

Blanchard, K., and S. Johnson, *One Minute Manager*. New York: William Morrow, 1982.

Deming, W. E. *Out of the Crisis*. Cambridge: Massachusetts Institute of Technology, Center for Advanced Engineering Study, 1986.

Iacocca, L., and W. Novak. *Iacocca: An Autobiography*. New York: Bantam, 1986.

Kume, H. *Statistical Methods for Quality Improvement*. Tokyo: The Association for Overseas Technical Scholarship, 1985.

Lewin, K. *Field Theory in Social Science*. London: Tavistock Publications, 1952.

Mizuno, S. *Company-wide Total Quality Control*. Tokyo: Asian Productivity Organization, 1988.

Parkenham-Walsh, S. and G. N. McLean. "An In-Process Model for Improving Quality Management Processes." *Consultation* 6, no. 3 (1987): 158-74.

Pasmore, W. A. *Designing Effective Organizations*. New York: John Wiley and Sons, 1988.

Persico, J., L. Bednarczyk and D. Negus. "The Role of the Union, Management and Consultant in a Total Quality Transformation Effort." *Continuous Improvement—The Challenge for the Nineties*. 43rd Annual Quality Congress Transactions. Milwaukee: American Society for Quality Control, 1989.

Peters, T., and R. H. Waterman, Jr. *In Search of Excellence: Lessons from America's Best Run Companies*. New York: Harper & Row, 1982.

Shewhart, W. A. *Statistical Method from the Viewpoint of Quality Control*. Edited by W.E. Deming. Washington, D.C.: U.S. Department of Agriculture, Graduate School, 1939.

Spencer, L. and J. Cullen. "A Literature Review in Taxonomy of Organization Development Research Variables and Methodologies." *Catalog of Selected Documents in Psychology*, Vol. 2. Boston: McBer and Company, 1981.

Tribus, M. "The Application of Quality Management Principles in Industrial Research and Development." *Quality First: Selected Papers on Quality and Productivity Improvement*, 157-63. 3rd ed. American Quality and Productivity Institute, 1987.

Turner, A. N. "Consulting is More Than Giving Advice." *Harvard Business Review* 60, no. 5 (September-October 1982): 120-129.

Biographical Notes and Acknowledgments

LORNE M. AMES, is president of the Manitoba Division of Inco Limited. He is an engineer with thirty years of operating experience. As head of the mining complex, he championed the implementation of quality management principles and the use of statistical process control. Mr. Ames believes the knowledge gained by trial and practice has application in all organizations.

GERRY (GUS) A. DAMON, is the TQM office manager at Pearl Harbor Naval Shipyard (PHNSY). He has a bachelors degree in mechanical engineering from Stanford University and a masters degree in psychology from the University of Northern Colorado. He has worked for Philco/Ford designing communications satellites, taught at the Hawaii Preparatory Academy, and was a member of the propulsion branch of design division at PHNSY. In 1981, he became the quality circles program manager and, in 1986, he began teaching process improvement as part of what was to become TQM. He has written articles about implementing TQM for the National Shipbuilding Research Program and *Quality Engineering* magazine.

Mr. Damon acknowledges Dr. John Persico of PMI as "a constant source of energy and knowledge and a passionate believer and translator of Dr. Deming and the TQM movement."

ROBERT KILLEEN, has spent forty years in the labor movement representing blue collar workers at the bargaining table and as an international representative and sub-regional director for the UAW in Minnesota. He credits former UAW president Walter Reuther for inspiring his efforts to create opportunities for worker involvement. In 1960, under his leadership as bargaining chairman, the Twin City Ford assembly plant was turned around through a union initiative. The plant was constantly recognized during the 1960s and 70s as one of Ford's best plants in quality and cost, and at the same time as one of the most respected, militant, and responsible local unions within the UAW. As a member of the governor's commission studying the economic future of Minnesota, Mr. Killeen was instrumental in forming the Minnesota Council for Quality, a privately funded nonprofit organization. Since retiring in 1988, he criss-crosses Minnesota lecturing management, labor, educators, and others on the principles of TQM and stresses that to successfully implement these programs they must be understood by the entire front-line workforce.

Mr. Killeen gives special thanks to Lou Schultz of PMI, Jim Buckman, executive director of the Minnesota Council for Quality, and Irv Bluestone, retired vice president of the UAW, for their help and support in understanding the quality movement.

SHARON K. LOUBERT, is a statistical consultant for PMI. Her responsibilities include providing direction and assistance with SPC applications, developing and implementing statistical training material, and working with senior management to plan and implement the overall quality improvement process. Dr. Loubert has worked in federal government and in the chemical, food, health care, and automotive industries at both management and engineering/technical levels.

Dr. Loubert previously worked as a manufacturing reliability engineer. She has completed research in the area of life data analysis with applications in product lifetime testing. She holds a B.A. in mathematics from St. Olaf College and an M.S. and Ph.D. in statistics from Iowa State University.

LAWRENCE A. LUCCHESI, is plant manager at the Chevron Chemical Company's Cedar Bayou Plant. Mr. Lucchesi earned his degree in chemical engineering at Auburn University, is a registered professional engineer, and now has thirty years' experience in the chemical process industry. He is a member of the Texas Chemical Council Executive Board and chairman of the Occupational Safety Committee, a member of the West Chambers County Chamber of Commerce and Baytown Chamber of Commerce, vice-chairman of the East Harris County Manufacturers Association, and a board member of the Baytown Economic Development Foundation and Houston Regional Monitoring Corporation.

JOHN PERSICO, JR., is an organizational development Consultant for PMI. He received his Ph.D. in training and organization development from the University of Minnesota. Dr. Persico works with PMI clients to help them develop total quality organizations by applying the Deming philosophy. He is a member of the American Society for Quality Control and the Institute of Management Consultants. He writes and speaks regularly on TQM topics, and his articles have appeared in *Quality Progress, Quality,* and the *TQM Journal.*

Dr. Persico has had previous experience as a retail store manager, a loan officer, and in both state and federal government.

JOHN B. ROGERS, is vice president of finance and treasurer of Zytec Corporation. Prior to joining Zytec in 1986, Mr. Rogers held positions in finance at Wagner Spray Tech and Dayton Hudson Corporation. He earned his M.B.A. in corporate finance from New York University, and has done post-graduate work at the University of Chicago.

Mr. Rogers' chapter on the Quality Leadership Team is a result of interviews with several key people at Zytec: Sharon Ockwig, Priscilla Klabunde, Rosemary Junker, Larry Matthews, Pat Hinderman, Robin Stegner, Pat O'Malley, and Roald Haugan.

LOUIS E. SCHULTZ, is chief executive officer and founder of PMI. He has thirty years of experience in marketing, product development, planning, and general management. Mr. Schultz is recognized internationally in the field of quality improvement, and PMI serves a wide spectrum of private and government organizations throughout North America and Europe.

He serves on the editorial board of *Human Systems Management,* is a member of the Asian Pacific Congress on Quality Control, an advisor to the North Central Deming User's Forum, a board member of the Minnesota Council for Quality, and a recipient of the 1987 Professional Partnership Award from the University of Minnesota. He is listed in *Who's Who in the Midwest* and *Who's Who in Finance and Industry.*

Mr. Schultz holds a B.S.E.E. from the University of Nebraska and an M.B.A. from Pepperdine University. He has written and published numerous articles about quality improvement and its application to industry and service organizations. He acknowledges Pat Morris for her critical perspective and editorial contributions that shaped the Introduction to this book.

DAWN L. SORENSON, has a B.A. in business and communications from the College of St. Catherine, and has studied organizational development, training, and statistics. She has applied her skills in the areas of teambuilding, leadership, strategic planning, and TQM in both profit and nonprofit organizations. She has been instrumental in assisting top management with creating organizational mission statements and designing and implementing organizational change. She has also conducted training in SPC, customer service, and supervisory skills in both union and nonunion environments.

Ms. Sorenson gives special thanks to the employees of the H. M. Smyth Company for the development of this information on teambuilding, and for their persistence in continual and constant improvement.

A. W. STEWART, is senior vice president of Dominion Bridge, a United Dominion Company. He is currently National Director and past Manitoba Chair of the Canadian Manufacturers' Association; director and current chairman, Total Quality Manitoba Inc.; director, Science/Technology Awareness Network, Manitoba (STAN); and chair of the Central Regional Committee of the Canadian Institute of Steel Construction.

Mr. Stewart is a registered Professional Engineer with a degree in civil engineering from the University of Manitoba. He has also attended the executive management program at Banff School of Advanced Management and the Amos Tuck School of Business.

The perspective in Chapter 2 is that of the Executive Steering Team established through team collaboration and comprised of A. W. Bischoff, E. G. Buchinski, P. F. Hunter, G. C. Koch, W. L. Moore, D. P. Negus, R. J. Partridge, M. P. Schioler, and A. W. Stewart. The team accepted the concept of variance even within itself and diligently worked to reduce it. In the final analysis, was the effort of Dominion Bridge people that made the difference, the team acknowledges.

MICHAEL S. THOMAS, is currently a district superintendent with Chevron Pipe Line Company (CPL). From 1988 to 1990, Mr. Thomas was the quality improvement coordinator for CPL, advising the Management Steering Committee in the start-up planning and implementation of the TQM transformation, and coordinating TQM training company-wide.

Mr. Thomas, a registered Professional Engineer, earned his B.S. in mechanical engineering from the University of California, Santa Barbara. He has worked for CPL for twelve years as an engineer, and in a variety of operating positions throughout CPL.

Mr. Thomas acknowledges the tremendous individual and team efforts of the hundreds of people who work to improve quality in CPL, especially the Process Improvement Advisors, the management team, and the consultants from Process Management International.

JOHN S. VOLLUM, as an account manager with PMI, Mr. Vollum works with clients to formulate, implement, and continually improve their quality improvement process. The central theme of this role is the establishment and improvement of a win-win client-consultant relationship.

Prior to joining PMI, Mr. Vollum spent ten years directing continuing education programs for engineers and scientists at the University of Minnesota. He also was a research consultant for the Minnesota House of Representatives, specializing in public policy and legislation relating to issues of environment and natural resources, workers' compensation, and healthcare. His other experience includes work with the United Nations Industrial Development Organization in Vienna, Austria.

Mr. Vollum holds a B.A. in philosophy and psychology from Gustavus Adolphus College, and an M.A. in education from the University of Chicago.

Index

Organizational Development
(OD) Consultant, *xxiv*,
118, 121–36
continuous improvement
phase, 133–36
implementation phase, 128–33
objectives, 121–22
planning phase, 122–25
Organization leader, *xvi*, 1–18,
19
commitment of, 72
and continuing improvement
plans, 13–15
and Organizational Development Consultant, 123
promoting improvement, 15–
17
role of, 3–5

P

PACE conference, 50
Pakenham-Walsh, Samuel, *x*
Pareto chart, 12, 35
Pay-for-knowledge concept, 65–
66
PDCA Cycle, *x–xi*, 68, 79, 85,
110, 114, 135
Pearl Harbor Naval Shipyard
(PHNSY), *xix*, 47–57, 132
Performance evaluation, 14–15,
136
of Process Improvement Ad-
visor, 86–87
of Process Improvement
Teams, 114
Persico, John, Jr., *xxiv*, 117–49
Personal appeals, 15–16
Personal profile, 110–11
PERT charts, 125
PIM Instructors. *See* Process Im-

provement Methods
(PIM) Instructor
Planning, 51–52
long range, 49
phase, 122–25
transformation, 140–41
Plant Advisors, 45
Plant Training Coordinator, 39
PMI. *See* Process Management
International
PMI Model, *ix–xxv*
basic stages, *xv–xvi*
structure and roles, *xiii–xiv*
see also individual components
(e.g., Organization
Leader, Executive Steer-
ing Committee, etc.)
Policy
management, 51, 131
reviewing, 38
Policy DIT (Deming Implementation Teams), 62, 65, 69
Practices DIT (Deming Implementation Teams), 62–63,
65, 69
Presentation skills, 85, 125
Pride, employee, 7
Principle management, 51
Priorities, setting, 68–69, 124,
131–32, 144
Problem solving, 7, 29, 89, 93,
94
Process Improvement (PI) Advisors, *xiii*, *xxii–xxiii*, 52,
75–100
and Applications Consultant,
87–93
and Internal Consultant, 96–
100
major responsibilities, 75
and Process Improvement
Consultants, 146